LADIES' SOUTHERN FLORIST

Mary Catherine Rion

LADIES' SOUTHERN FLORIST

BY MARY C. RION

A FACSIMILE OF THE 1860 EDITION

WITH NEW INTRODUCTIONS BY

JAMES R. COTHRAN AND
DEBRA MCCOY-MASSEY

University of South Carolina Press

© 2001 University of South Carolina

Published in Columbia, South Carolina, by the
University of South Carolina Press

Manufactured in the United States of America

05   04   03   02   01   5   4   3   2   1

Library of Congress Cataloging-in-Publication Data

Rion, Mary C. (Mary Catherine), 1826–1901.
  Ladies Southern florist : a facsimile of the 1860 edition / by Mary C.
Rion with new introductions by James R. Cothran and Debra
McCoy-Massey.
      p.   cm.
  Originally published: Columbia, S.C. : P.B. Glass, 1860. With new
introd.
    Includes bibliographical references (p.   ).
    ISBN 1-57003-420-6
    1. Flower gardening—Southern States. 2. Plants, Ornamental—
Southern States. I. Title.
SB405.5.S68 R56   2001
635.9'0975—dc21   2001041440

Following page 138 is a facsimile of the 1860 publications catalog of P. B.
Glass of Columbia, S.C., the original publisher of *Ladies' Southern Florist*. The
catalog, containing an advertisement for the book, was included in the first
edition and is reproduced here for its value in social and publishing history.

The editors and the Press wish to thank the Cherokee Garden Library of the
Atlanta History Center for providing the original edition of this book, from
which the facsimile was made.

Dedicated to Anne Coppedge Carr,
Founder, Cherokee Garden Library,
Atlanta History Center

CONTENTS

———

BOOKS FOR SOUTHERN GARDENERS

———

Prior to the nineteenth century, southern gardeners had little in the way of instructional material to provide advice and recommendations on ornamental gardening. With the exception of agricultural and commercial almanacs and two early garden guides—*The Gardener's Kalendar* by Martha Logan in 1779 and *The Gardener's Calendar for South-Carolina* by Robert Squibb in 1787—southerners had to rely almost exclusively on English garden books for advice on planting schedules, procedures, practices, and design. While the material contained in English garden books proved useful to a limited degree, much of the information provided was inappropriate for the unique growing conditions of the southern states. Before 1800 several of the more important English garden books known and used by southern gardeners included: A.-J. Dézallier d'Argenville's *The Theory and Practice of Gardening* (1709, translated from French into English by John James in 1712), Philip Miller's *The Gardeners Dictionary* (1740–1743), Thomas Whately's *Observations on Modern Gardening* (1771), and Thomas Mawe and John Abercrombie's *Every Man His Own Gardener* (1794).

It was not until the beginning of the nineteenth century that American garden books first appeared on the scene. The earliest of these, *The American Gardener* (1804) by John Gardiner and David Hepburn, and *The American Gardener's Calendar* (1806) by Bernard M'Mahon, were soon followed by additional works that addressed topics ranging from the cultivation of fruits, vegetables, vines, flowers, and ornamental plants to the construction of greenhouses, cold frames, and hothouses of various sizes and designs. Interestingly, all but a few of these early works were compiled and written by American nurserymen. Nurserymen possessed the greatest knowledge of plants and seeds that were adaptable to local conditions, and they desired to provide American gardeners with the necessary information to stimulate growth and expansion of the American nursery trade.

As most early American garden books were written by northern nurserymen in Philadelphia, New York, and Boston, instructional material relating to specific needs of the southern gardener remained almost nonexistent until the time of the Civil War. One of the earliest attempts to rectify this deficiency was undertaken by Francis S. Holmes in the preparation of *The Southern Farmer and Market Gardener,* published in Charleston, S.C., in 1842. The author's primary objective was to collect material from both European and northern sources and, using his personal experience and observations, adapt it to the growing conditions of the lower South. While Holmes's efforts were directed primarily at the cultivation of fruits and vegetables in the South Carolina lowcountry, it represented the first comprehensive effort by a southern author to provide specialized instruction specifically directed to the unique growing conditions of a region characterized by mild winters, a long growing season, high humidity, and extended periods of heat and drought.

The Southern Gardener and Receipt-Book, published in 1845 by Phineas Thornton, a nurseryman in Camden, S.C., with more than forty years of practical experience, provided southerners with another book on gardening. While the book focuses mainly on fruit and vegetable gardening, additional topics such as cooking, beverages, dairy, medical, veterinary, and other miscellaneous subjects are also included. After Thornton's death, a revised edition was printed by Mary L. Edgeworth of Fort Valley, Ga., and published by the Philadelphia firm J. B. Lippincott in 1859. Edgeworth notes that the title is somewhat deceiving as its usefulness was in no way limited to the South but was "equally applicable to all sections of the Country with some little variation in time, dependent on latitude and climate."

It was not until 1856, with the publication of William Nathaniel White's *Gardening for the South,* that southerners were provided a garden book that included advice for cultivating vegetables, fruit trees, and a selected list of ornamentals "adapted to the states of the Union, south of Pennsylvania." A native of New York, White relocated to Athens, Ga., in 1847, where he combined his literary skills as editor of various agricultural journals with his personal knowledge of gardening to produce a practical publication that was adapted to the climate, habits, and requirements of the South. In his preface White states, "If this treatise, with all its imperfections, shall in any degree increase the love of Gardening among us; if it shall cause orchards to flourish, shade-trees to embower, and flowers to spring up around any southern home, the author's purpose is accomplished."

The first garden book published in the South prior to the Civil War that dealt exclusively with ornamentals was Mary Catherine Rion's *Ladies' Southern Florist*. Not only was *Ladies' Southern Florist* the first garden book written specifically on ornamentals for southern gardens, but it was also the earliest garden book of its kind in the South written by a woman. Published in Columbia, S.C., in 1860, this small but informative book was intended to provide every lady of education in the South a garden book that was not only practical in nature but also easily understood. As Rion notes in the preface, her primary objective was to produce a work "on Flower Gardening which might be adapted to the South, written in a manner as to be intelligible to one not a *professional Florist*" (her italics). Like other authors of the period, Rion combined her personal gardening experience with that contained in prominent garden books of the times, including: Robert Buist's *American Flower Garden Directory* (1839), Joseph Breck's *The Flower-Garden* (1851), and Alexander Watson's *The American Home Garden* (1859).

Ladies' Southern Florist is an important and pivotal work in southern garden literature in that it was the earliest garden book in the South written by a woman and the first definitive work to offer gardeners a comprehensive list of trees, shrubs, flowers, bulbs, and roses ideally suited to the southern climate. While Rion references each plant by its common name (rather than using botanical nomenclature), there is seldom doubt in the mind of the reader as to the plants she describes. It was her intention to avoid all technical and scientific terms so that her work could be easily understood and enjoyed by all. In addition to a general description of each plant, Rion provides a wealth of practical information on gardening, including planting schedules, soil preparation, maintenance procedures, watering requirements, and propagation techniques—primarily based on her personal experience as an avid gardener. *Ladies' Southern Florist* reads as pleasantly today as it did 140 years ago.

Of the more than 150 plants described in *Ladies' Southern Florist,* many are traditional favorites that southern gardeners have known and loved for years—magnolia, box, cherry laurel, oleander, Carolina jasmine, marigold, jonquil, daffodil, hollyhock, larkspur, four-o'clock, and roses. In addition, a large number of entries are newly introduced plants from China and Japan. Many of these selections gained immediate popularity in the South both for their unusual foliage and flowers and for their adaptability to the unique growing conditions of the southern climate. Some of the more important of these newly introduced Asian plants described by Rion include: blotch plant (*Aucuba japonica*), camellia (*Camellia japonica*), gardenia (*Gardenia jasminoides*), enonymous (*Enonymous japonica*), Chinese magnolia (*Magnolia obovata*), crape myrtle (*Lagerstroemia indica*), fragrant olive (*Osmanthus fragrans*), pittosporum (*Pittosporum tobira*), tea plant (*Thea sinensis*) and azalea (*Azalea indica*). Many of these introductions are still treasured by southern gardeners.

With a growing interest in historic gardens and heirloom plants, *Ladies' Southern Florist* is an excellent source of information on ornamental plants and gardening prior to 1860. Whether employed as a guide for the selection of time-tested plants for use in contemporary gardens or for instructions in organizing and planting a flower garden, *Ladies' Southern Florist* transcends time by conveying the joys, pleasures, and challenges associated with gardening in the South that are as relevant today as they were in Mary Catherine Rion's time.

JAMES R. COTHRAN
LANDSCAPE ARCHITECT/GARDEN HISTORIAN

MARY CATHERINE WEIR RION, 1829–1901

Mary Catherine Weir was born March 16, 1829, in Sparta, Ga., to Samuel Weir, Jr., and Margaret Weaver Weir, who, along with their younger son, George, had moved south from Harrisburg, Pa., in the late 1820s. Shortly after Mary Catherine's birth, Samuel Weir relocated his family to the Camden/Lancaster area of South Carolina, where he assumed the editorship of several local newspapers. A third child, Margaret Elizabeth, was born to the Weirs in 1833. Around 1840 Samuel Weir moved to Columbia, S.C., to become editor of the *Southern Chronicle*. Prior to that time Samuel and his wife had separated, presumably because of religious differences or philosophical conflicts over social conditions in the South. Following their separation, Margaret Weir returned to Pennsylvania with their youngest daughter, leaving Mary Catherine and George to live with their father in South Carolina.

Mary Catherine grew up in the South during a period when education was highly valued for young ladies of the privileged class. Academic training was available from private schools or tutors in botany, plant collecting, and gardening, as well as the classical subjects of art, music, Greek, Latin, and

French. From all accounts, Mary Catherine was offered many educational opportunities and proved to be an excellent student. In addition to a formal education, Mary Catherine was exposed during her early and adolescent years to many of her father's professional friends who were members of Columbia's social and intellectual elite.

Samuel Weir died in 1847, several months after Mary Catherine's eighteenth birthday. Following the death of her father, Mary Catherine was invited to live at the home of William Campbell Preston, president of South Carolina College (today the University of South Carolina). Mary Catherine resided there for several years during which time she had the opportunity to visit Preston's sister-in-law (daughter of Wade Hampton), Caroline Hampton Preston, who at the time was living with her widowed mother, Mary Cantey Hampton, who was purported as having one of the finest ornamental gardens in Columbia. The garden is described in *Gardens of Colony and State* (1931–1934) by Alice Lockwood as "filled with shrubbery and flowers of costly varieties." Mrs. Hampton's garden, no doubt, stimulated Mary Catherine's interest in plants, gardening, and landscape design.

While living at the home of William Preston, Mary Catherine met her future husband, James Henry Rion, a scholarship student at South Carolina College. Born on April 17, 1828, James Rion was the son of Henry and Margaret Hunter Rion of Montreal. Henry Rion had died the month before James was born. Following her husband's death, Margaret Rion moved to Savannah where she served as the housekeeper for the Pulaski Inn. James attended the Chatham Academy for several years, excelling in math and history. At the age of fourteen James and his mother relocated to Pendleton, S.C., where his education continued at the Pendleton Male Academy. Shortly after the move, Margaret Rion was employed as the housekeeper at Fort Hill, the home of John C. Calhoun, noted statesman and powerful South Carolina senator. James's classmates at the Pendleton Male Academy included three of John Calhoun's sons—John, James, and William. James Rion developed a close relationship with the Calhoun family, including Calhoun's eldest daughter, Anna Maria Calhoun Clemson and her husband, Thomas Clemson, founder of Clemson College, the first agricultural college in South Carolina. James Rion had a broad range of interests, including agriculture, horticulture, and landscape design. He was instrumental in the design of Bonaventure Cemetery in Savannah and experimented with the growing of tea.

James Henry Rion and Mary Catherine Weir were married on December 11, 1851, at the home of Mary Catherine's uncle, J. W. Weir, in Harrisburg, Pa. That same year, James accepted a position teaching math, history, and military science at the Mount Zion Institute in Winnsboro, S.C. In 1854 James passed the bar and began practicing law. In addition to developing a successful law practice, he served as president of the Planters Bank of Fairfield, owned a granite quarry, and was involved in a number of businesses in the surrounding area. Winnsboro served as the Rions' hometown throughout their thirty-five-year marriage, during which time they raised nine children: Preston, Margaret Hunter, Floride Calhoun, Kitty, William Calhoun, Holbrook, Lucy Tenney, John Weir, and Hanna. In 1857 the Rions purchased a two-story home on South Congress Street. In addition to her responsibilities as a wife and mother, Mary Catherine found time to indulge her interest in the pleasurable pursuit of gardening. Not only was gardening an acceptable activity for educated women in terms of artistic expression, but it was also promoted as a benefit to one's health and an escape from the rigors and demands of daily life.

From all accounts, Mary Catherine laid out her ornamental garden in a traditional manner with a central walk bordered with dwarf boxwood (*Buxus sempervirens suffruticosa*), complemented on either side by symmetrically placed trees. The entire garden was enclosed by a decorative fence behind which was planted a clipped hedge of cherry laurel (*Prunus caroliniana*) hedge. Within this layout, Mary Catherine set out to add a flower garden. Finding little in the way of advice on preparing and planting a flower garden that would flourish in the South, Mary Catherine decided to combine her own knowledge of gardening with that found in works of northern authors to produce *Ladies' Southern Florist.*

Published in 1860, on the eve of the Civil War, this small but informative book was intended to provide ladies in the South with a practical work on flower gardening that was written in a simple style that was informative, easily understood, and specifically adapted to the unique growing conditions of the southern climate. *Ladies' Southern Florist* was well received as noted in the July 1862 issue of the *Yorkville Press:* "It tells in plain language how to plant flowers, when and where; how to dig, trench, hoe, manure, prune and water flowers; how to kill bugs, caterpillars and worms; how to manage cuttings, buddings and hundreds of other similar things. There is fifty times as much common sense in this little book on flowers—on Southern flowers be it remembered—as we have ever seen in anything of the kind." While a second edition of *Ladies' Southern Florist* took place the same year of its initial publication, additional printing was cut short by the Civil War.

Mary Catherine was afforded little time to enjoy the accolades and praise received as author of *Ladies' Southern Florist,* for shortly after its publication South Carolina seceded from the Union and for the next several years was deeply involved in the Civil War. James served as a colonel for the South while Mary Catherine played an important role in the successful exchange of Union and Confederate prisoners. In return for her efforts, the Rions' home and property were spared by Gen. William T. Sherman and his forces in the final days of the war.

Following the death of James in 1886, Mary Catherine experienced a deep sense of personal loss. It was during this period that Mary Catherine established a close relationship with her youngest daughter, Hanna, a painter, writer, and accomplished musician. The bond between the two was reinforced through their mutual interest in flowers and gardens. In 1894 Mary Catherine accompanied Hanna to Europe on a

concert tour. During the trip Mary Catherine wrote enthusi-
astically of people, the opera, and many sites in Europe.
Upon returning home, Mary Catherine spent her remaining
years with Hanna in Reading, Pa., until her death in 1901.

Hanna's interest in gardens and her writing skills led to
the publication of two garden books, *The Garden in the Wilderness* (1909) and *Let's Make a Flower Garden* (1912). In *The Garden in the Wilderness* Hanna writes of returning to Winnsboro
to visit her mother's garden in hopes of seeing "the beautiful
old tracery of paths and the curves of symmetrical beds," only
to find "universal neglect." While little remained of Mary
Catherine's once beautiful garden, Hanna recalls its memories in the "legacy of words" so clearly written and described
by her mother in *Ladies' Southern Florist*. The reprinting of
this important work after 140 years will once again allow
Mary Catherine's garden to bloom as it reaches a new generation of gardeners who will delight in its content, benefit
from its advice, and share in the pleasures of gardening in
the South.

DEBRA MCCOY-MASSEY, M.A.
HERITAGE PRESERVATION

LADIES' SOUTHERN FLORIST

LADIES'

SOUTHERN FLORIST.

BY

MARY C. RION.

"This is an art which does mend Nature,—change it rather: but the art itself is Nature."—SHAKSPEARE.

COLUMBIA, S. C.:
PETER B. GLASS.

1860.

Printed by C. P. Pelham, Columbia, S. C.

PREFACE.

The Author of this volume, desiring a book on Flower Gardening which might be adapted to the South, and, at the same time, written in such a manner as to be intelligible to one not a *professional Florist*, was unable to find any work answering either of these requisites. After procuring such works on Flowers as were accessible, I commenced making memorandums of such information as I found in these, by observation, to be suited to our climate—making such modifications, corrections and additions as my experience suggested. These memorandums I enlarged by inquiries made of practical flower-garden *workmen*, and by hints derived solely from my own practice.

The works on Flowers to which I have referred, are those of Buist, Breck and Watson. I also consulted the Patent Office Reports, and other valuable Congressional publications. By these means, my memorandums, intended solely for my own use, assumed quite formidable dimensions. A friend, happening to look over them, suggested that I should have them published in book form, if for no other reason than for my own convenience. In following this suggestion, which I have done after some hesitation, I am alone actuated by a desire to place in the hands of the Ladies of the South such a work as I in vain sought, when I commenced the culture of my Flower Garden. If I accomplish this, it is all I desire.

I have intentionally avoided all technical or scientific terms, using only those understood by every lady of education. In some of my directions I have been very precise and minute, in order that I might avoid that defect of all works on Floriculture that I have ever seen, of giving directions in such a manner as to be understood only by those who needed no instruction on the subject.

I have omitted many plants, because they either required no particular culture or were well known to every one; and my aim was to make a *small* Hand-Book of Flowers.

M. C. R.

Winnsboro', S. C., Feb. 22, 1860.

Ladies' Southern Florist.

BOTANICAL OUTLINE.

Every lady who has a flower garden should be sufficiently well acquainted with botanical terms, to express herself intelligibly about the different plants and flowers she cultivates. We give such distinctive terms as may serve this purpose, furnishing a botanical vocabulary that one may properly use in conversation without appearing pedantic.

Plants are *woody*, as the rose, or *herbaceous* as the pink. According to the size, woody plants are *trees* or *shrubs*. Woody plants have solid stems, like the rose; or hollow stems, like the golden rod. Herbaceous plants are *bulbous* rooted, like the hyacinth; *tuberous* rooted, like the dahlia; or *fibrous* rooted, like the pink.

With regard to duration, those plants that mature and die the *first* year, are termed *annuals;* those which mature and die the *second* year, are *biennials;* while those which live an indefinite number of years are termed *perennials.* Thus the phlox is an annual—the holly-hock is a biennial—and the rose is a perennial. Trees and shrubs generally are perennial.

Leaves are *orbicular,* or round, like the nasturtion; *reniform,* or kidney-shaped, like the ground ivy; *cordate,* or heart-shaped, like the heart-leaved aster; *oval,* like some of the azaleas; *elliptical,* like the olive; *lanceolate,* like the peach; *linear,* like the gladiolus; *acerose,* or needle-shaped, like the pine; *palmate,* or hand-shaped, like the passion-flower; *digitate,* or finger-shaped, like the parts of the peonia leaf; and *tubular,* like the side-saddle flower. The margins of leaves are *regular; serrated,* or notched like a saw; *crenate,* or scalloped; *ciliate,* or fringed like the eye-lashes; *lobed,* when deeply indented; and *prickled.* Leaves are also *simple,* like the olive, or *compound,* like the peony or rose.

According to the duration of the leaves, plants are termed *caducous,* that is, those whose leaves fall before the end of summer; *deciduous,* or dropping the foliage in the autumn; and *evergreen,* whose leaves preserve their greenness throughout the year. Most evergreens change their leaves annually, but the new foliage is always sufficiently developed before the old ones fall, to preserve the verdure. Those evergreens that do not change their leaves annually, but renew their foliage but once in two, three or more years, are called *persistent* evergreens.

According to Botanists, all plants have flowers; but, in common parlance, those only are called flowering whose flowers are conspicuous or ornamental.

The different parts of a flower are well worthy close examination. Let us examine the divisions of the pink. The flower leaves, upon which the color of the pink depends, are called *petals ;* all the petals of a flower, taken together, form the *corolla*. In the single pink, the corolla consists of five petals—in the morning-glory of only one petal. Those flowers which have a single row of petals, botanists style *natural,* while they contemn those which have two or more rows of petals, as *monsters*. We think that a better nomenclature, would be that of *natural* and *improved*. We would designate a single pink as natural, and a double pink (the botanist's monster) as an improved variety.

Within the petals are little thread-like organs ; the two central ones are *pistils*. The end of the pistil is called the *stigma ;* the part of the flower out of which the pistils grow is called the *germ ;* the part of the pistil, between the germ and the stigma, is the *style*. The germ, when mature, has one or more *cells*, which contain the seed. The ten thread-like organs that surround the two pistils, are the *stamens*. The little head to a stamen is the *anther ;* this bursts, when the pink comes to maturity, and scatters a fine light dust which it contains, called the *pollen*. It is the pollen, falling upon the stigma of a flower, that fructifies it, or causes the production of fruit or seed. The pollen of one flower, carried by the wind or insects to the stigma of other flowers, under favorable circumstances, produces mixed varieties, or hybrids. Botanists style the stamens, the male organs, and the pistils, the female organs of plants.

The number of pistils and stamens differ, and are variously combined and situated in different flowers. Upon this depends the Linnæan system of Botany, once considered the best, but now superseded by what is styled the Natural system. As words are arranged in a dictionary, according to the letters which they contain, without regard to their meaning, so Linnæus placed in the same class those plants whose flowers had the same number of pistils and stamens, without the least respect to their other characteristics. Thus, according to Linnæus, the pink and the hydrangea belong to the same order and class. Botanists now classify plants according to their physiological peculiarities and diversities of external and internal structure.

The petals of a pink are bound together by a green envelope; this is the *calyx*. Some flowers, the lily for instance, have no calyx.

PREPARATION OF THE GARDEN.

———

When it is within one's means, or time allows of the delay, *trenching* is undoubtedly the best of all preparations for a flower garden. Thorough trenching and manuring will amply repay all labor and expense, by the rapid and luxuriant growth of every thing. But often this is not practicable, and in such cases we recommend the process of "garden-trenching" as a very good preparation of the soil for planting. This is done as follows: Commence on one side of the garden, two feet⁻ from the fence, and dig a trench one spade deep, throwing the earth on the side towards the fence. Then manure the bottom of this trench and spade up the bottom, turning it over and breaking up the subsoil with the spade,

2

mixing in the manure with the subsoil. This done, commence a second trench, alongside the first, likewise digging one spade deep and throwing this earth over into the first trench. Then manure the bottom of the second trench, and spade it in as in the first. Then begin another row, and continue the process until your whole garden ground is thus trenched. A very important advantage in this plan of digging, is the preservation of the surface soil on top, while at the same time the subsoil is loosened and enriched. After the last trench is finished, have the earth, which was thrown next to the fence out of the first trench, carried over to fill up the last trench on the opposite side of the garden. When it is known where wide walks are to be, the manuring may be dispensed with in such places, though the subsoiling must be carried on throughout. Be careful to eradicate every vestige of grass roots while thus trenching the garden. Having finished trenching, rake the surface even and lay out the garden into walks and beds. This done, scatter over the beds woods' earth, or such other manure as you may wish to enrich the surface soil with. Allow the ground to settle a week or ten days before planting any thing.

Every one must suit their own taste as to the *plan* or design of the flower garden, as no rule can be laid down for this. The main walk, from the dwelling to the front entrance, should be the width of the steps of the house; and, in long walks, the width should be increased in proportion to the length. Beds should never be square or triangular, but they should be oval, or circular, or irregular in shape. Edgings to the beds, to keep them in shape, can be made of dwarf box, violets, lavender, pinks, and lemon or vanilla grass. The beds should only have a slight elevation above the walks, which will soon be attained by the depression of the walks, caused by treading upon them.

Ornamental hedges along the main walk, or on the sides and rear of the garden, are handsome and appropriate. But, unless you wish to conceal your garden from view, never plant a hedge in *front*. Hedges may be grown of wild orange, privet, French furze, euonymous, and tree box, of green or variegated varieties.

If the situation is sloping and liable to wash by rains, the garden should be laid out in terraces. This is picturesque, and the *only mode* by which such gardens can have any permanency. The face of these terraces may be made permanent and ornamental by being sodded with vanilla or ribbon grass, or both combined.

In furnishing plants for your garden, let the opposite sides correspond without being identical. For instance, a rose on one side may correspond with a rose on the opposite side, of a different color. Match an evergreen by an evergreen opposite, of the same character, but of a different variety; an English laurel by a magnolia; a deodar cypress by a funereal cypress, etc. By such an arrangement, you will not, as some thoughtlessly do, reduce your garden, as far as variety goes, to one half its extent. As a general rule, making an exception only in favor of the most beautiful and showy varieties, have only *one* of a kind, which, if it dies or meets with an accident, you can replace from the same source you obtained that one.

It is better to procure plants, of all kinds, from a nursery as near you as possible, as they will be assimilated more to the locality you reside in. Never import plants from a more northern clime, as the process of acclimation is difficult and always hazardous.

HEDGES.

It is of the greatest importance to prepare the ground thoroughly for hedges, to bring them sooner to maturity, and to make them more durable. The ground should be trenched two or three feet deep, throwing the subsoil on one side, and the surface soil on the other. If the soil is poor, it is absolutely important to manure well, mixing the surface soil and the subsoil with the manure, layer by layer, until within a half foot of the level of the ground. Then fill up with surface soil, mixed with woods' earth. Allow the trench to settle before planting, and fill up again, if below the surrounding surface. For the first two years the hedges must be kept free from weeds. Trim them close and neat, and clip, both on the sides and top, once or twice a year. They should be trimmed just before the new growth starts. Always clip in a conical or elliptical form, as the thinning of the branches towards the top increases the development of the plants at the bottom, in consequence of the greater elaboration of sap in those parts, and the free admission of air, light and rain.

The *Arbor-vitæ* is valuable for hedges, on account of the beauty of its foliage and compactness of its growth. Planted alternately in two rows, from twenty to twenty-four inches apart. In a few years the hedge increases so much in thickness as to become impenetrable.

The *Laurustinus*, with its shining leaves and showy white flowers, is very easily cultivated, and makes a beautiful hedge. It is difficult to keep this hedge in tolerable shape, on account of the luxuriant shoots which it sends out. It should be pruned with a knife. Prune early in the spring, cutting out those shoots that have already flowered, cutting close to a leaf. But the new shoots of the spring must not be shortened in, because the flowers are produced at the extremity of the new wood.

Of the *wild orange, French furze, tree box, euonymous,* etc., for hedges, we treat particularly elsewhere.

The *Cherokee,* or the *Mac Cartney* roses, are admirable for fences, planting the cuttings a foot apart and six inches deep, leaving one end out, pointing to the south. Press the earth closely to them with the foot. If properly pruned they make beautiful and impenetrable hedges. The Cherokee requires constant shortening in, or it will die out at the bottom, and become unsightly, in which respect it is much inferior to the single white MacCartney rose. The last rose must have rooted cuttings to prove entirely successful. Both roses are of most rapid and luxuriant growth.

The *lilac* makes a pretty hedge alternated with the *sweet brier,* but they are not evergreen. The sweet brier seed should be sown in the spring, having kept them in sand through the winter. Let the plants grow as they like for the first year. The second year cut them down to the ground and they will spring up and require no further care than occasional trimming. When the stalks become naked, cut the roses down to the ground again.

TRANSPLANTING.

This should never be done when the earth is so wet that it adheres to the spade, but only when the soil is friable. Dry, cool weather—cool, but not freezing—is the best time. Transplanting may be done any time from the middle of September to the middle of February. The early spring is the most favorable season for all shrubs, just *before* the new growth starts. The shorter time the plants are out of the ground, the surer of success is the operation of transplanting. If you are not prepared to plant immediately, bury the plants, slanting to the south, in the ground until you are ready. Cut off with a sharp knife any bruised roots, and prune irregularly grown branches. Never cut away the tops of any resinous evergreen. Evergreens are best removed in early spring. These are apt to suffer by winter transfer.

Climbing shrubs should be cut down to the ground in transplanting, that the growth may be entirely new. The same plan is good for the laurel, which is an exception to its kind. Plants or shrubs from the woods should be closely pruned, cutting away from the head of the plant (except in evergreens,) one-third to one-half its height, carefully shortening and opening. In taking up plants, care should be taken to secure good roots and to bring away all the fibres as perfect as you can. Deciduous shrubs should not be transplanted after the leaves begin to expand.

The following process will be found excellent for transplanting. Dig a hole two
or three feet square, and eighteen inches or
two feet deep, according to size of plant.
After manuring the bottom with well-rotted
manure and earth mould, well incorporated
with a portion of the soil, place in the roots,
and fill in gradually with finely pulverized
earth, placing the transplant *above* the level
of the surrounding ground, to allow for set-
tling. Set the plant with the same side to
the south which it preserved in its former
location. This, in most plants, can easily be
recognised, as the leaves always present
their face to the south, while the back of
the leaf is towards the north. After filling
up the hole, raise a circular ridge around
the plant, so as to form a basin into the
stem. Then slowly pour on water, until the
ground will soak up no more without over-
running the ridge. Let the earth settle for
half an hour; then fill in and rake the sur-

face even. Support the plant with a stake until it is established. Shade and keep moist until it rains, and then let the plant take care of itself.

SEED-SOWING.

The soil on which flower seeds are to be sown should be rich and light, and prepared with great care, being finely pulverized and then pressed with a board. Seed should be sown from one-eighth to an inch deep, according to size. The smallest seed should be scattered on the surface, and then fine soil strewn or sifted evenly over, not covering more than an eighth of an inch deep. Press the top again with a board. Protect from the sun by evergreen boughs, and water freely until well up.

In sowing seed for the purpose of procuring improved varieties, care should be had, not only that the seed are taken from the finest existing kinds, but also from the handsomest, the largest and the most perfect specimens, and these alone should supply future seed.

Seed planted in the winter remain in a torpid condition, and will come out as soon as the warmth of spring is felt. The seeds of most *annuals*, or such plants as live but one year, should be planted in the spring, while many biennials require to be planted in the autumn to be vigorous.

Flower seed to be sown in the *Spring :*— China Asters, Poppy, Petunia, Portulacca, Morning Glory, Coxcomb, Larkspur, Heartsease, Holly-hock, Sweet William, Phlox, Mullen Pink, Indian Creeper (very late), Bachelor's Button, Candy Tuft, Clarkia, Ice Plant, Mignonette, Ambrosia, Tasselflower, Sensitive Plant, Anemone, Sweet Pea, Amaranth, Feverfew, Fringed Gentian, Iris, Pinks, Sun Flower (very late), Marigold, Calliopsis, Ladies' Slipper, Gilly Flower, Verbena.

3

About the 23d of March is the best time
for sowing all the above seed, except the
more hardy, which may be sown at the time
of the flowering of the peach. If the season be unfavorable and cold after the sowing of the seed, the seed-beds should be
covered with boards to retard the vegetation until all danger is past. As soon as
the boards are removed the seed will come
up rapidly, and only require moisture to
thrive.

Flower seed to be sown in the *Fall:*—Cor-
copsis, Canterbury Bells, Fox-glove, Mourn-
ing Bride, Snap-dragon, Candy Tuft, Four-
o'clocks, Double Rocket Larkspur, Columbine, Gladiolus, Clematis, Periwinkle, Violet, Forget-me-not, Love-in-a-mist.

Some of these flowers give stronger plants
by *fall* planting, though *spring* planting will
give earlier blooms. The middle of October is the time to sow all the above flower
seed.

WATERING.

This operation, unless done very judiciously, is likely to effect more harm than good. The blooming of most plants is improved by copious watering during their season of flowering; but this should only be tried with the healthy and vigorous ones. During times of drought, in hot weather, many sickly plants are killed by injudicious watering. For these, the best medicine is *shade*. Shingles, boxes with the top off and one end knocked out, or matting on stakes, will answer for this purpose, using one or the other, according to the size of the plant. *With* shading, water properly applied is beneficial in hot, dry seasons; and without shading, is positively injurious, unless the application be very copious, so as to saturate the ground to some distance from the plant, and be repeated daily. In *cool*, dry weather, watering is more apt to be beneficial. All

plants have the power of adapting themselves to the season, and it is a bad rule to
water merely because the weather is dry.
Except in the case of *recent* transplants, and
cuttings *lately* established, as a general rule
never water.

When necessity requires watering, observe
the following rules :

1st. In cold weather, water in the morning after sunrise, with cold water.

2d. In hot weather, use water that has
been standing in the sun all day, or made
warm by adding hot water, and apply after
sundown.

3d. In hot weather, unite shading with
watering.

4th. Use a watering pot with a finely
punctured rose, and holding it close to the
plant, shake it while watering, so that the
drops will fall scattering, as when raining.
By this method you avoid hardening the

ground, and more water is absorbed by the soil immediately around the plant.

5th. Where shading is impracticable, and the weather hot, dig a hole with a trowel as near the stalk as the roots will allow and pour water in this hole until it will absorb no more, *allowing none to touch the plant itself*. The next morning fill up this hole with earth.

6th. Where rule fourth is followed, unless the surface around the plant is covered with *mulch*, the next morning stir the ground around the stalk.

These rules are in conflict with those usually given, but trial will prove them correct. The non-observance of the second rule has caused the loss of many a rare and costly plant.

As germain to this subject, we would state that we have found it an excellent rule, not to dig or hoe the garden during a drought; where weeds appear, remove them by hand. Digging up the ground, during hot dry weather, causes it to lose whatever of moisture there may be left.

ROSES.

The *Rose* has been very appropriately styled the "Queen of Flowers." This rank it has long, and will, perhaps, forever maintain. A fine assortment of the best varieties of this flower would alone make a handsome flower garden.

The rose will succeed well in any soil, but to have *fine* roses great care in cultivation is necessary. *Our* climate is most congenial to the rose, and with us it can be brought to the greatest perfection. To South Carolina the world is indebted for some of the finest roses that grow.

The soil should be deeply dug and enriched with well-rotted manure. *Poudrette* (night-soil deodorized with charcoal dust,) is one of the best manures for the rose. Well

rotted hen-house manure, mixed with dirt
from the wood-pile, is a valuable application.
Charcoal dust is an excellent surface dressing; it imbibes and retains moisture, keeps
the plant healthy, and intensifies the color of
the *red* varieties. A dry sandy loam is the
best soil: wet or stiff clay soil is injurious;
and where these drawbacks exist they should
be remedied by drainage, and the admixture of sand and woods-earth and leached
ashes.

Rose bushes may be planted from late in
the fall to early in the spring, just before
the buds swell; always selecting a dry and
cool day. All broken or bruised parts of
either the limbs or roots should be cut off
smoothly with a sharp knife. *Every* rose
should be supported by a suitable stake and
neatly tied to it. The *climbers* require frames.
Follow the directions elsewhere given for
Transplanting, observing that roses removed
in the spring should be pruned more closely

than those planted in the fall. For the first year after planting the stalk should be surrounded by *mulch*, that is, coarse litter, straw, moss, dead weeds or grass; this should be kept in its place for awhile by small rocks.

The bushes should be examined daily, and any catapillers or lady-bugs found upon them killed. As to the rose-bug, patronize *toads* for their destruction. The green rose louse will not injure the plant, unless they become very numerous, in which case they can be killed by smoking with tobacco, covering the whole bush with a sheet at the time.

Unless you desire to multiply the variety, all suckers should be cut away as they make their appearance. Those roses which send up many suckers should be lifted every three or four years, the roots thinned out, and then replanted. As any limbs die or turn yellow, promptly cut them away, cutting down into the healthy wood.

During the flowering season, the development of the blooms is aided by frequent watering. Liquid manure applied in the evening, not upon the plant, nor in contact with it, but around the surface soil, from the time the first bud commences to open until the blooming season is over, greatly enhances the size and brilliancy of the flowers. When the rose-buds are formed in large numbers, and open slowly, they should be freely thinned out, to increase the vigor of those left. When the rose blooms in clusters, a superb single flower can be produced by pinching off all the flower-buds save the largest, at the time when the buds are *distinctly developed*. Roses of Cloth of Gold of double ordinary size can be thus produced. As soon as the blooms wither, cut them away, as the formation of the seed is a great drain on the vigor of the plant, and besides, withered flowers mar the beauty of the bush.

Pruning of roses should be done in the

fall or spring, cutting away old wood and the feeble growth of the last year. The different varieties of roses require different pruning : directions will be given under appropriate heads. Never attempt to change the character or habits of roses; adapt your pruning to the particular kind of rose.

TEA ROSES.

These roses are so called from their fresh tea fragrance, which most of them have. They are generally of light, delicate colors. The finest of this class are Triomphe of Luxembourg, Devoniensis, La Pactole, La Marque, Safrona, Aurora Tea, Eliza Sauvage, Joan of Arc, Marshal Buguead, Smithii, Caroline Tea, and the *Noisettes*. This subdivision of the tea roses are hybrids, produced by a French Florist named Noisette, who cultivated a nursery in Charleston about fifty years since. When first produced they caused great excitement among the Parisian florists, and for years Cloth of Gold plants commanded the price of *five dollars* all over the United States. The choicest of the Noisettes are the Cloth of Gold, Solfatare, Glorie de Dijon, Ophire, and Charles the Tenth. The *Isabella Grey* is also classed with the Noisettes, being a hybrid between the Cloth of Gold and the Persian Yellow, produced by Mr. Grey, of Charleston, about ten years ago. This rose resembles Cloth of Gold, but is of a deeper yellow, and when first introduced the French Government sent an agent to Charleston to buy up, at a premium, all the plants which could be obtained.

BOURBON ROSES.

This class of roses is admirably well suited to our climate, luxuriating under the burning heat of a tropical sun. The originals of this class were first produced on the Isle of Bourbon; hence the name. They are almost perpetually in bloom from April to November, and with few exceptions are highly fragrant. These qualities, together with the symmetrical form of the flowers, render this class highly desirable for our gardens. These roses require deep and rich soil to bloom freely. They succeed well, either on their own roots or budded. The finest of the Bourbons are: Souvenir de Malmaison, Madame Desprez, George IV., Mrs. Bosanquet, Marshal Villars, Queen of the Bourbons, Paul Joseph, Leveson Gower.

HYBRID PERPETUALS.

This is a comparatively new class of roses, and bloom twice a year, in the spring and fall. These roses are very difficult to establish, and so long a time being required before the layers can be disengaged from the old plants, (being *two* years,) that budding is generally resorted to for propagating them. This is the reason why these roses are always bought from the nursery-man on budded stocks. They neither succeed so well, nor do justice to themselves in regard to blooming, on their own roots. On budded stocks they produce the finest flowers. Of the *hybrid perpetuals* the select ones are: Madame Laffay, Baronne Prevost, Duchess de Nemours, La Reine, Crimson Perpetual, Duchess of Sutherland, Emperor Napoleon, Marshal Raglan, Lion of Combats, Baronne Halez, Giant of Battles, Prince Albert, Glorie of Lyons. Hybrid perpetuals should be severely pruned in the *spring*, if a fine autumn display is desired. To have early spring flowers, prune very sparingly in the fall.

CHINA ROSES.

These are perpetual bloomers, and thrive admirably in our climate, being too tender for a more northern latitude. They require a dry, loamy soil. In trimming these, never *shorten in*—only thin out the shoots. They flower best on the young wood. This ap-

4

plies also to the Tea and Bourbon varieties. Of the China roses the choicest are: Madame Bosanquet, Grandiflora, Louis Philippe, Cinnamon, Damask, China Triumphans, Agripina, and Madame Desprez.

MOSS ROSES.

These are extremely lovely in the bud, and the red and blush are beautiful when full blown. They are rather difficult to transplant, and must not be pruned at all, except to cut away dead wood. The only method of propagating the moss rose is by suckers or layers. The white roses of this class are not desirable.

MUSK ROSES.

The leaves of the musk rose are delightful perfume for clothing. For this purpose the flower leaves should be gathered early in the morning.

BRIER ROSES.

Of these the *sweet brier* should find a place in every garden, for its exquisite fragrance. The *Harrison* is a fine yellow variety, of luxuriant growth. It is excellent for an arbor or fence rose, but too rampant for a bush, though we have seen the long branches gracefully festooned over the main bush. The suckers are troublesome, and this rose can be abundantly multiplied from them. Prune only the old wood of this rose, and that sparingly. The new growth should not be touched, as it bears the flowers. The *Persian yellow* is a still finer variety of the same—deeper in color, and a very desirable rose. This rose is decidedly improved by budding on a China rose stock, doing better than on its own standard. *Fortune's yellow* is a showy rose, of a rich salmon color, a single flower, but gay and ornamental. It can be propagated by cuttings; but it is of slow growth until fully established, when it becomes very luxuriant. This rose should never be shortened in, and requires only little pruning.

CLIMBING ROSES.

These are not a distinct class, but belong to the preceding ones, being those which have climbing habits. They thrive best on deep, rich soil. The hole for climbers should be dug two feet square, and enriched to the depth of two feet, in order to sustain their luxuriant growth. In the fall they should have a top dressing of manure and woods' earth, which should be dug in very early in the spring.

The pruning of climbers requires more judgment than that of other roses. The two years' old wood does not produce fine flowers; hence, the new growth must be encouraged and the old wood cut away, preserving, however, the main stem the whole length. Prune the lateral branches, in the fall, to one or two buds; this will make finer flowers.

The best of the climbers are: The La Marque, the Banksias (which are evergreen), Cloth of Gold, Baronne Prevost, Glorie de Dijon, Cora L. Barton, the Prairie Queen, Multiflora, and the Greville rose. All of these are suitable for frames, porches and arbors.

ROSE CUTTINGS.

Rose cuttings may be planted at any time, when the buds are plump, if care be taken to water and shade when the weather is hot. From the middle of December to the middle of February is, however, the best time. The choice cuttings are those which form the extreme of the stems, and have a leaf bud on the end. From these, of course, nothing must be cut off the upper end. If there are any leaves on the cutting, trim them off at once, leaving the whole of the leaf-stem. The cuttings should be from four to six inches long, according to the diameter of the cutting. Cut off with a very sharp knife, very near and below the lower bud, commencing on the side oppo- site that bud, and slanting downwards. Cut the top off, half way between the top bud and the next one above it.

In choosing a situation for the cutting plantation, select the north side of a house, fence or piazza. Make the soil, as far as the cuttings reach, pure sand—the purer and cleaner the better. Thrust a garden trowel down slanting, so that the cutting will lean towards the south; draw out the trowel, and insert the cutting so that the bud next to the top bud will be just under the sur- face, turning the upper part of the top bud to the north. Holding the cutting with the left hand, thrust in the trowel on the north of the cutting and prize it, while in the

ground, *against* the *cutting*—this will pack
the sand tightly against the cutting. Then
draw out the trowel, and fill up the hole it
leaves.

Plant the rows of cuttings from east to
west, six inches apart; and where you plant
more than one row, plant each succeeding
row on the north of the one already planted.

After planting, if you can obtain charcoal
dust, scatter enough over the surface to fill
up the unevenness made by planting. Or,
if this is not to be procured, make the
ground even with the hand, and cover the
surface over with pine or other short straw,
being careful to leave the ends of the cuttings uncovered. This done, water freely at
once, unless the weather is freezing at night,
in which case water sparingly next morning,
when the sun softens the ground.

Keep the ground slightly moist until a
rain; after which, never water unless the
weather is very dry. Mark the names of

the roses in each row by a stick with a label, lest you forget the names of your cuttings. If these directions for planting be strictly followed, the failure of a single cutting will be accidental.

After the cuttings begin to grow, select the shoot of most upright growth, and with a sharp knife cut off all other shoots as they make their appearance. If the bud which is just beneath the surface sends up a shoot, let this be the one selected, as it will make a well formed bush. As any *flower-buds* make their appearance, pinch them off, as they retard the wood growth. Keep the beds clear of weeds and grass, which must be done by the hand.

When the bushes are one year old, transplant where designed to stand, being careful to place the side which has had most exposure to the sun towards the south. After the hole which is to receive the rose bush is dug, and the roots are put in their

position, run down a small rod, not inter-
fering with any of the roots, to which tie
the stem. Then fill in with finely pulverized earth, and follow directions elsewhere
given for *Transplanting*.

BUDDING ROSES.

Budding may be done at any time when
plump buds can be procured, and the bark
easily slips from the stock on which you are
to bud. The best season for budding is
from June to August, and should be done
late in the afternoon.

As soon as you cut the stem on which are
the buds you will use, at once trim off all
of the leaves, leaving the whole of the leaf-
stem; otherwise the leaves will be pumping
out the moisture from the cutting as long
as they are left on it. Cut the bud from
the stem with a sharp knife, commencing
about a third of an inch above the bud,
passing nearly half through the stem, and

coming out one-half an inch below the bud.
Then take out the wood, by commencing
at the lower part and bending it out gradually upwards, supporting the wood with the
thumb-nail, so that the eye of the bud will
not be torn out. As soon as this is done,
put the bud in your mouth, to keep it moist.

Now make a horizontal incision half way
around the stalk of the stock, through the
bark to the wood. From the middle of this
incision make a perpendicular cut down,
three quarters of an inch in length. With
the back of the blade, gently separate the
bark from the wood on the two sides of the
perpendicular incision. Take the bud out
of your mouth and insert it into the incision, between the bark and wood, and force
it down as far as it will go. Then cut off
the bark above the bud, exactly over the
horizontal cut made in the stock. This will
make the bark above the bud exactly fit
the bark above the horizontal incision on

the stock. With coarse woollen yarn bind around the stalk, commencing at the lowest extremity of the perpendicular cut and proceeding upwards, also wrapping above the bud. Tie the yarn in a bow-knot, that it may be loosened when necessary.

After the inserted bud has grown about half an inch, unwrap the thread, and rewrap it more loosely and wider apart than before. As soon as the bud commences to swell, cut off the stock an inch above the bud.

For *stock roses* select the Dog or Dutchman rose, or vigorous young shoots of the Mycrophilla. Bud low down on the stock (except where rose trees are desired), within two or three inches of the ground, and put the bud in on the north side of the stock. All thorns on the bark of the stock, near where the incision is to be made, should be broken out with the back of the knife before commencing to bud.

When the bud has attained a growth of four or five inches, place a rod on the south side of the stock, close against it, and bind the shoot to the rod with a strip of cloth, occasionally tightening the strip; and, as the shoot grows, put on additional strips. By these means you will secure an upright growth, a handsome tree, and prevent the new shoot from being broken out by the wind. After the shoot has attained the height of five or six inches, cut the portion of the stock which has been allowed to remain above the bud, close off to the bud, slanting the cut upwards, from the south side. This cut will bark over during the summer, and the stock and bud have the appearance of a uniform growth.

CUTTINGS.

All other cuttings may be propagated according to the method given for rose cuttings, except in resinous evergreens, or

those which have rough leaves, like the cedar. The cuttings of these should be taken
from the *ends* only, preserving the tip end,
cutting off the laterals with a sharp knife.
The cutting thus prepared should be planted
three-fourths of its length below the surface,
and placed *perpendicularly*, instead of slanting, in the ground.

Cuttings of evergreens and shrubs should
be planted early in the spring, when the
leaf-buds are well developed, just before
bursting.

HYACINTHS.

In October prepare the ground for these
bulbs, by digging two feet deep, thoroughly
mixing with the soil, as it is returned, equal
parts of earth mould and well rotted manure and clean sand. A small quantity of
poudrette, put in deep, is beneficial. Pulver-
ize and mix in the earth thoroughly with
the manure. Then cover four inches thick

5

with sand, that the manure may not touch the bulbs.

Plant the bulbs of the hyacinths a month after preparing. It is better to plant them in November, because they are weakened, like all other bulbs, by being kept out of the ground too long; and the blooming is stronger when planted in the fall. When planted in the spring, or in January, they are *forced* before they are matured, and do not bloom well.

Plant the bulbs three inches deep in the sand. The colors are believed to mix by planting the different colors together; therefore one should sacrifice beauty of display for the permanent beauty of the colors, by planting the different colors in separate groups.

The bulbs should be set eight inches apart. If the soil is too light, bulbs will be injured by the heat. If too clayey, they will grow feebly and seldom bear handsome flowers.

Four months after blooming, the foliage dies or turns yellow, when (the spot having been previously marked by sticks with labels) the bulbs should be lifted and separated. The small offsets should be replanted *at once*, to grow for next year, which is better for them than drying. Lift the bulbs when the ground is dry.

Keep all the colors distinct, and carefully wrap each in a bit of newspaper, and bundle all in paper and mark them. Then put away in a room where a fire is never built. We have pursued the newspaper plan of preserving hyacinths for years, and never lost one.

The *double* varieties are considered finest, but the *single* kinds often make up in the increased number of bells. While blooming, the surface soil around the hyacinths should be kept friable with a light hoe.

Red hyacinths range from deep crimson to the most delicate shade of pink.

Blue hyacinths run through several shades, from a purple to the most delicate tint of blue.

Yellow have but three shades—straw, cream and saffron.

White hyacinths are distinguished by red, blue, purple, and yellow and green eyes, and sometimes by green stripes.

Feathered hyacinths are much more hardy, and require less culture, than the garden hyacinth. They can be easily cultivated on any light, loamy soil, without extra attention. They have a musky perfume, and should be cultivated in masses.

Prepare hyacinth beds a little rounded, in order to shed off water; too much moisture will rot the bulbs. Never allow seed vessels to form (unless you wish to experiment on new varieties), as they weaken the root and injure the succession of bloom.

TULIPS.

These bulbs thrive best in moderately poor soil, and they will do very well on any ordinary sandy soil, without extra preparation. However, some pains-taking will be rewarded by an improvement. The soil may be spaded twenty inches deep, and, being thoroughly pulverized, mix *at the bottom* a very little well-rotted manure—about one-eighth of the whole soil. A top dressing of four inches of pure sand having been given, the bulbs must be planted three inches deep, *in dry weather*.

The proper time for planting tulip bulbs is in October, or November, at latest. If kept out of the ground, they, of all other bulbs, are weakened, and do not bloom so finely. In lifting the bulbs, the flowering or old roots should be wrapped in paper, labelled and put away in a dry, cool place, until it is time to plant out again.

The offsets, or small bulbs, should be

planted out again, to grow and strengthen until fall, when they can be removed to the tulip-bed. In the tulip the new bulbs form *under* the old ones, and these, if permitted to remain several years in the ground without lifting and separating, become so weakened that they will not flower at all. Therefore, tulip bulbs should be taken up at least every two years, and the finer kinds every year. Set the bulbs out in groups of four or five of each sort, and the effect will be much finer. The larger bulbs should be planted a little deeper than the smaller ones.

Tulips are liable to a change in color, which is called *running*, by which the beauty of the tint is lost in a muddy color. This is prevented, and the original color preserved, by taking up the bulbs as soon as the foliage dies, and drying and setting out again in the fall. Do not allow any seed vessels to form, as they exhaust the root and spoil the succession of blooms.

The *double* tulips are coarse, formless, and generally thick-colored. With two or three exceptions, they are hardly worth cultivating. The graceful form of the natural flower is its great beauty. The double rose scented, the golden centred crimson, and the bright red striped, are very beautiful.

PEONIAS.

Dig fifteen inches deep in a rich, light garden soil, and manure well in the bottom, finely pulverizing and mixing the soil. A northern and a sheltered situation is best for this plant. Transplant in October, and set the crown of the root three inches below the surface. They do not flower well when transplanted in the spring, when the fibres are pushing forward. A top dressing of coarse stable manure in the fall will make them flower more handsomely in the spring. Chop it in carefully very early in the spring, not injuring the crown of the plant. Under high cultivation, there are often produced, on one plant, from fifty to a hundred magnificent flowers.

The peonia is propagated by division of the root, and sometimes by suckers. By layers, also, they may be propagated, by bending down the shoots in the spring and confining them with pegs. These shoots are very brittle, and they should be fastened with great care. The peonia is in bloom three months of the year, and therefore very desirable in the flower garden.

Two years in the same situation is as long as peonias should be allowed to stand. Lift the roots, divide and reset them in new soil in the fall.

TUBEROSES.

These exquisite plants require very rich loam. Only strongly grown roots will flower; consequently, the careful preparation of the soil is important. Spade the ground two feet deep and enrich with well-rotted manure, leaf mould and *poudrette*. Prepare the ground a month before needed, in the spring. On a dry day, in the latter part of February, plant the bulbs two inches deep in the ground, pressing the earth to them. Plant the offsets separately, to produce flowering roots for the next year, as the bulbs seldom produce flowers the second time.

As soon as their foliage dies the bulbs should be lifted, and, being divested of the dead foliage and fibres, put away in newspaper or dry sand. Plant again in the spring. They are very tender, and liable to be killed if planted too early. There are single and double varieties, of the most delicious perfume. The flowers are borne on a stalk from three to five feet high, which requires the support of a stake.

WHITE LILY.

This lovely plant grows in clusters, adorning with its drooping head the garden walk, and charming with its sweet perfume. The best time to transplant it is just after it is through its flowering season, in the late spring. It does not do well if removed early in the spring, after the vegetation has started. It is not beneficial to the lily to remove often. Lilies should be cultivated in groups of from three to eight. A top dressing of coarse stable manure, in the fall, will make the lily bloom stronger in the spring. Work in the manure in the early spring.

Herbaceous plants, such as lilies, pinks, peonias, etc., should not be allowed to grow into too large stools. They should be lifted, and fresh soil given, every two or three years. Set the roots a little deeper than before, as the tendency of such plants is to grow out of the soil, when allowed to stand long in one place. In two weeks they will root again, and should be occasionally watered, if the weather is dry.

The *tiger* lily is very rich and showy, and produces its bulbs in the axil of the leaves, from which new plants can easily be produced. Sow them as soon as ripe.

DAFFODILS, JONQUILS, IRIS, CROCUS, SNOWDROP.

All of these bulbs should be transplanted in the fall, while they are dormant. The bulbs should be planted two and a-half inches deep, in light rich soil, though they will grow in any soil not too stiff.

All bulbs delight in *sandy* soil. Separate the roots every three or four years, leaving them in the ground during the winter. Cultivate all of these plants in clusters, for effect. A handsome arrangement of them can be made in waves, circles, and various figures, by close and uniform planting.

GLADIOLUS.

This is the wild corn-flag of Italy. This bulb requires deep preparation of the soil, being of a vigorous growth. Rich sandy soil is most suitable for its cultivation.

The bulbs are like the crocus, and, like it, the new bulbs grow *above* the old ones, and, being too near the surface, are very easily killed by the cold; therefore, they should be taken up and separated every two years, to prevent this.

Plant the *seed* in the spring, and transplant in the fall. The bulbs must be planted a few weeks earlier than the tuberoses, and require high culture to flower handsomely. Dig up the roots when the foliage dies, and keep them cool and dry until the next spring.

HOLLYHOCK.

Some gardeners prefer the double Chinese hollyhock to the prim and more stately dahlia.   Cultivated from the *seed*, this flower will bloom in two years.   It dies out the third year, if the roots are not divided.   Sow the seed late in the spring, and transplant from the seed bed.   It is a coarse, strong-growing plant, requiring rich soil; but the flowers are very showy, and the plant easily cultivated.

Transplant the seedlings late in the summer.   The next year, when it blooms, destroy all plants bearing inferior flowers.   Select the finest, and propagate by dividing the roots every year, just after flowering, cutting off all young shoots.   Cultivate in groups.   Finer varieties of hollyhock are sometimes increased by cuttings made from the eyes of the flower stems.

CHRYSANTHEMUMS.

These bloom in October; hence their common name of "October pinks."   It is highly improved in blooming by reducing the num-

6

ber of flower buds on each shoot to one or
two. In May or June the plants should be
properly trimmed and bushed, but not later
than this. Tie up the bushes to stakes, where
not upright and independent, in the month
of September. This will preserve the flowers from being ruined by wind and rain.

The different colors should be kept distinct, or all will eventually change and run
into one muddy hue. The colors and forms
are various, from the large double to the tiny
button size, of the most exquisite form and
tint.

They are easily propagated by division of
roots in early spring. Finer blooming plants,
however, can be reared from cuttings than
by division. Cuttings must be made just
after the blooming season is over.

The situation of chrysanthemums should
be changed every three years, or the earth
around them entirely renewed by fresh soil.
Pig manure is excellent for the chrysanthe-

mum, as also hen manure, applied very early in the spring.

SPIRÆA.

The various *white* spiræas are easily cultivated in any garden soil, but strong, rich, moist soil is most suitable for their perfection. Stiffness in the soil is necessary to them.

Propagate by suckers, division of roots and layers.

The *Douglass* spiræa is not at all like the class, and has a dirty pink grass-like bloom. It is not worthy a place in any garden, and is exceedingly troublesome with suckers.

LAGERSTREMIA, OR CRAPE MYRTLE.

This may be readily grown by cuttings or suckers. No particular pains is necessary in the culture. It is improved by close winter pruning, and should be pruned only in the winter. Cut away the wood of last year to within two or three eyes of the wood of the preceding year. By this plan you will secure the finest and largest spikes of flowers.

SYRINGA, OR MOCK ORANGE.

The flower buds are very beautiful, resembling the orange blossoms. It will thrive in any garden soil, and can easily be increased from suckers.

Thin out the old wood in the winter, and cut out the weaker of the new shoots.

FLOWERING ALMOND.

Early in bloom, and one of the few early bloomers in pink color. It is very hardy, and can be abundantly multiplied by suckers. Prune into shape in the fall, and keep down the suckers during the summer. It should be more cultivated.

AZALEAS.

This genus of highly ornamental shrubs are, many of them, indigenous with us,

being known as the wild honeysuckle.
The colors vary from white to a deep
red, which last is rare. The azalea is a
flower of great elegance, and not difficult
of culture in this its native clime, if
some attention be paid to give it a good
situation and suitable soil. Azaleas require
moist, black, sandy loam, and a *shady*
situation. If the wild azaleas are procured from the woods, they should be cut
down to the ground, and they will send
up numerous shoots and form fine healthy
plants. No *animal manure* should ever be
applied to an azalea. During the heat
of the first summer, after planting, they
should be shaded by pine boughs placed
upon the south side.

Azaleas may be freely raised from seed,
or from layers and suckers. They require
water while blooming, to have them in
perfection. Rocks laid about them will

conduce to retaining the moisture of the soil.

The Chinese and Indian varieties require protection during very cold weather. Boughs or coarse litter will answer this purpose.

RANUNCULUS.

This splendid plant requires the soil to be trenched eighteen or twenty inches, and enriched with earth mould, a little well-rotted cow manure, and an admixture of clay and sand throughout. The root of the ranunculus is a cluster of small tubers, like claws, united in the crown, which should be planted an inch and a half under ground—deeper planting is injurious. After the plant appears, it should be kept weeded, and the soil pressed firmly around them after they get two inches high. They require watering during drought. The best situation for the ranunculus is a cool and moist one.

Care should be taken to secure sound and plump roots. As soon as the foliage dies the roots should be lifted and thoroughly dried, and put away in a cool and dry place.

GERANIUMS.

These can be cultivated in the open air in our Southern gardens. Plant cuttings under glass early in April. In a month or six weeks these will be rooted, when the pot should be emptied, keeping the earth entire, and the plant placed in a rather shaded situation. These cuttings will grow vigorously, and bloom through the summer, if moved carefully. In the fall, cut them down to the ground. Raise over the root, before frost, a small mound of coarse litter, which remove in the following spring when there is no longer danger of frost, and they will flourish again.

Earth mould is most suitable to enrich the soil for geraniums. The best variety for out-doors is the rose geranium, though many others are quite vigorous.

The heliotrope, so sweet and lovely, can also be grown out of doors in the same manner.

LAVENDER.

Although this is a common herb, it is not unworthy a place in a corner of the flower garden. It is a dwarf shrub, with delicate, glaucous foliage, and bears spikes of blue flowers, in June. The whole plant is delightfully fragrant, but particularly the flowers. These, gathered before the dew is exhaled, can be made up in neat and tasteful bunches, which delightfully perfume drawers and clothing. Lavender is easily propagated by cuttings or slips.

COLUMBINE.

This is finest when planted in masses. This elegant vernal flower is much improved by cultivation. The columbine can be propagated from seed, or the choice varieties by division of the roots. The root should be divided soon after flowering, and not in the spring. It will grow in any garden soil.

EVERLASTING PEA.

This plant is a most beautiful, large, light purple or pink flowering climbing perennial. It grows six feet high.

The pea may be propagated by dividing the roots, but sowing seed is the most usual mode. The seed should be planted where the plant is to stand, as it sends down a tap-root to a great depth. Young plants will flower the second year feebly, but the third or fourth year they produce a profusion of foliage and flowers.

SNOWBERRY,

Or, *wax-berry*, as it is often called. This plant is inconspicuous in flower, but is cultivated for its fine white berries, which grow in clusters. Propagate by suckers. It does best in a shady situation.

FOUR O'CLOCKS

Are interesting as well as ornamental flowers. Their roots are tuberous, like the dahlia, and can be multiplied and preserved by these tubers. They can, also, be raised from seed.

NANKIN PERILLA,

A singular herbaceous plant, growing two or three feet high, with branching stems well covered with ample foliage of a very dark purple hue. The flowers are small and numerous, but producing little effect. The strange color of the foliage is the principal ornamental merit, and contrasts finely with other plants. It is not abundantly self sowing, therefore the seed should be gathered, and sown in April. It is handsome, planted in masses, when its sombre hue contrasts agreeably with the brighter tints of other flowers.

ICE PLANT.

This is a singular, tender annual plant, with thick fleshy leaves, which have the appearance of being covered with very heavy dew. The young seedlings, if transplanted, should be planted in the same kind of soil in which the seed were sown. They can be turned into the open ground in May.

CHILI JASMINE.

This beautiful climber is a native of South America. The flowers are white, and of exquisite fragrance, growing in clusters. The bloom is produced on the extremity of the shoots. After the flowering season, the plants should be pruned back to within a few eyes of the wood of the preceding year.

SUMMER HELIOTROPE.

This is a lovely little annual, with sky blue bunches of feathery looking flowers, and is very ornamental planted in masses.

WALL-FLOWER.

The varieties are numerous, but the single is the most common, and exquisitely fragrant and gay. These last are abundantly self sowing in the fall, but the *double* varieties should be propagated by cuttings in the spring, placed in sand. The old bushes should be pruned in the fall, or they become scragly and unsightly.

The wall flower is a half-shrub evergreen. Light rich soil is best adapted to its culture, but it will thrive any where. Those with rusty brown streaks are considered finest.

GILLY-FLOWER.

The stock-gilly is deservedly a favorite. It can only be propagated by seed. It blooms the second year, therefore seed should be sown every year to keep up a succession of flowers. It is easy to transplant. The distance of the plants apart must be six inches. The soil should be very rich, and finely worked. The seed are very small, and must be carefully raked in when sown. It is an ornamental plant in a garden, in all its varieties of color.

7

PETUNIAS

Are ever-blooming, hardy annuals, of great variety of color. They are in flower from May to November. They should be planted in masses, and are showy trained over rock-work.

Single plants can be trained over small frames, and should always have supports, as they are trailing. The stems and leaves are covered with a viscid substance, which is unpleasant to the touch, therefore they are not suitable for bouquets, but they are handsome decorations to the flower garden.

They can be propagated from cuttings, but they must be protected during the winter. Double varieties are inferior to single.

PHLOX.

This is a perennial herbaceous plant, very handsome and showy, cultivated in masses. They require a shady situation and some moisture to thrive well. They will die out in dry situations.

They delight in a rich, light, sandy loam. When the plants become large, they should be divided, and planted in fresh ground. The phlox is in flower early, and is continuous in bloom until frost. They will continue longer in bloom by cutting down, after flowering, to prevent them seeding. If you wish seedling plants on the same spot, this trimming must be dispensed with, as the next seeding will be but imperfect. Sow the seed in the fall or spring.

PORTULACCA.

This is only a variety of the weed *pursley*. But, notwithstanding, when planted in masses, it is very ornamental. It looks well on rock-work and in jars, or in bordering for beds. The color is crimson, opening its bloom with the morning sun and closing at sunset. Sow the seed in the spring.

MIGNONETTE.

A bed of this should be planted in every flower garden, for its exquisite perfume. It can be kept in bloom all summer by trimming off the flowers to prevent them seeding. Sow the seed in the spring.

AMBROSIA.

This is also very fragrant. The long spikes of green bloom are very handsome in bouquets. It grows very large by cultivation in rich, moist soil. Sow the seed in the spring. It is abundantly self-sowing after being once established.

SNAP-DRAGON.

An imperfect perennial, which is apt to die out every few years. It is self-sowing after once being established.

Sow the seed in the fall, or in a hot-bed very early in the spring. Some varieties are very handsome. The *yellow* is objectionable, on account of its weedy propensity. Snap-Dragons will bloom the first year if sown in the fall. They can afterwards be propagated by division of the root or cuttings. The second year the flowers are finer.

The soil should be a rich, sandy loam, though in heavy, moist earth they will grow with greater vigor, but will not flower so profusely as in dryer and lighter soils.

CANTERBURY BELLS.

A biennial, which should be sown in the spring, and transplanted in August or September, where it is intended to bloom. The flowering is weakened by transplanting in the spring. The same effect of spring transplanting applies to all biennials, and most seedling perennials. No manure should be used on canterbury bells.

COREOPSIS.

A common, but showy plant. Sow the seed in the fall, and transplant in March, and it will bloom in June. Propagate afterwards by division of the root. It requires deep, black loam soil, and requires moisture for successful cultivation.

LARKSPUR.

The annual larkspurs are very hardy, and are best when self-sown in the summer. Sow the seed in September.

Rich, stiff soil is best suited to its culture. The seed must be sown where desired to stand, as they are injured by transplanting.

Thin out to stand six inches apart. Sow in masses.

Like many hardy annuals, seed sown late in the autumn will produce stronger plants, though the spring-sown seed may start out of the ground earlier. The lying dormant under ground during the winter seems to start the plants with more vigor, and they are more robust than the spring seedlings.

The *double rocket larkspur*, planted in a variety of colors, in masses, when in bloom is almost equal to a bed of a hyacinths. These seed must always be planted in the fall.

PINK.

Pinks can be grown from the seed, and are often abundantly self-sown. The carnations seldom bear seed. Seedlings often produce inferior bloomers, which should at once be exterminated, as they will injure the finer plants. This is especially the case with the carnations.

The *carnation* pink has preëminence in color and perfume. It is often handsomely striped; but the *French carnations* are pure in color, excepting sometimes they are mottled or pied. The *Florida* pink is a fine large mottled variety, but very tender, and scarcely bears our winter out of doors.

The *grass* pink is hardy and strong-growing, and is very showy and highly ornamental on borders of beds as edgings. But pinks are too exhausting for this purpose, injuring every thing growing within a yard of them.

Pinks die out in two or three years if left to themselves, especially the carnations. Propagate new plants by cuttings or pipings in November. Strip off the old leaves and, with a sharp knife, cut off the stem close below the joint of the stem. Trim the leaves and set the piping in sandy, dry soil, two inches deep. If planted in clayey or wet soil, they are apt to rot, and take root with difficulty. After planting the piping, press the earth to it with the thumb and finger, and keep moist until a rain.

The pipings will be ready to transplant in six weeks, and will bloom the same year. Old plants should have the earth renewed about every two years, and, trimming off all but three or four centre stems, replant about two inches deeper than before. The trimmings will do for pipings.

Hen-house manure sifted, and soot, are excellent for all pinks.

Sweet Williams are very lovely, and not so much cultivated as they should be.

GOLDEN ROD.

A deciduous shrub, of pithy growth. It attains the height of three or four feet. Like the spiræa and almond, the bloom precedes the leaves. The stems are covered with golden yellow bells, blooming the first of March. It is very showy and graceful. It can be easily increased by cuttings or suckers.

DOUBLE SUN-FLOWER.

Sow the seed late in the spring. This is a superb flower, nearly double the size of a dahlia, and quite as handsome in appearance. It should be more cultivated.

CANDY TUFT.

It is enlivening to the garden, planted in masses. It is hardy, and easily cultivated from seed. The finer varieties require to be propagated by cuttings. Spring-sown seed will do tolerably well, but autumn is the proper time to sow.

POPPY.

The poppy blooms three years from the seedlings. It is *impossible* to transplant them, therefore they must be planted where they will remain. Propagate, afterwards, by division of the roots, as soon as the foliage dies. If deferred until spring, the bloom will be weakly.

The poppy grows best in rich, stiff soil. Plant in masses.

FEVERFEW.

These are worthless, from *seed;* but raised from cuttings, or division of the root, are highly ornamental in the flower yard. Will thrive in any soil.

PERIWINKLE.

A trailing evergreen, flourishing best under shade and drip of trees. The flowers are of a pale blue, which, through its dark green foliage, is very cheerful. It can easily be propagated by cuttings, and is continuous in blooming.

VIOLETS.

Of these fragrant flowers, the *Tuscan* variety is the finest. Violets grow best in the shade. They should be divided, and the soil renewed entirely every two years, to continue blooming. If neglected, they will grow. to vines and flower but sparingly.

They should have no heating manures. All that is necessary to their successful culture is wood dirt, or earth mould. Violets make good borders to beds in shady situations.

The division of the roots should be made in the fall. Cultivate in large patches. The violet can be propagated by the seed, which are contained in seed vessels beneath the leaves, close to the ground. These are formed after the violets are through blooming in the summer. Sow the seed in the fall.

HEARTSEASE.

An annual, self-sowing, and very much improved by culture. Vegetable manure is best for this, too. They require shade to do well. Only the darkest and richest bloomers should be kept, and all others destroyed.

PANSEYS.

These are an improved variety of heartsease. The seed are only good for *one* year, deteriorating by keeping. They should be planted in a protected situation, and sheltered in winter. Moisture is destructive to the pansey, and they should be shaded from the hot sun. The same plant seldom blooms twice.

The finest panseys should be marked for seed and cuttings. Cut off at the second or third joint, and insert two inches deep in a light, sandy soil, and they will root in a few weeks. Remove all blighted leaves

8

immediately. The soil should be moderately rich with vegetable mould, and kept stirred frequently around the plant.

MALLOWS.

These are a species of showy plants, of easy culture. They can be propagated by seed or division of the root.

HORNED POPPY.

The particular beauty of this plant is not its flowers, which are pretty—but its "sea-green, dew-splangled leaves." It is a biennial.

MULLEN PINK.

A common, showy border flower, which is not a perfect perennial, but easily kept by dividing the root. The seed will bring flowers the second year. It blooms in April or May.

ANEMONE.

This is a delicate little plant of the early spring. Its flowers are bluish purple or white. It should be planted in a shady, sheltered spot.

AMARANTHUS TRI-COLOR.

This is an old but very handsome plant. It grows three feet high, and its foliage is its great beauty. Every leaf is striped with red and yellow, white and green. It is, really, one of the most ornamental stalks I have ever seen. It requires good soil and depth, and plenty of room, to excel.

TASSEL-FLOWER.

A graceful flowering annual, waving its crimson tassels throughout the summer.

BALSAMS.

For raising the double kinds, *old seed* are considered the best. Seed should only be gathered from the double flowering. They require rich soil and much moisture, in a shady situation, to produce fine plants and a profusion of flowers. They are highly ornamental, in the varieties of color, to the garden. Plants can be raised from seed, layers or suckers.

Balsams, China asters, marigolds, ten week stocks, hibiscus and zinnias, and most of those plants of a free growing and strong wooded nature, do best by transplanting.

BALSAM OF APPLE.

This is an annual. It is a climber, four feet high, and bears yellow flowers. The fruit is fleshy and ovate, and red when ripe. It grows well in this climate, and the fruit is preserved in brandy for the cure of cuts and bruises. It should be cultivated for this virtue, if one were not interested in the curious plant. It should have a stout support, four feet high.

RHODODENDRON.

This is the American Rose Bay, and grows fifteen or twenty feet high. The foliage is evergreen, leaves large and beautiful, oval, and partially renewed every three or four years.

There is small chance of any of the trees growing which are brought from the woods, because they come from swamp lands. The seed will come up readily, but it requires time and patience to bring it into flower. Shade and humidity are indispensable to this shrub's growth. It requires light rich soil, and moisture.

CHINA ASTERS.

The seed, when sown in the fall, produce very early flowers. But spring sowing brings on finer blooms in the summer. Transplant a month after they appear above the ground. Black loam is best adapted to its culture and perfection.

COCKSCOMB.

Save seed only from the finest combs. Sow them in very early spring in a hot-bed. Transplant, and as it grows, remove the side branches to produce one strong head. The *crimson* is only worthy of cultivation, the white being a dirty and inconspicuous color.

The soil for the cockscomb cannot be too rich to bring it to perfection. Fresh horse-dung, without litter, and green turf, watered abundantly, and a shady situation, will bring gigantic and magnificent combs —a handsome ornament to any garden.

CYPRESS VINE.

A native vine, of exquisite beauty. The seed are difficult to germinate, but are abundantly self-sowing when once established. Scald the seed, and let them remain soaking in water a few days, and when planted they will soon come up. They are very weedy when once planted, and troublesome on that account.

The cypress vine is rather difficult to transplant. Seed do best when sown where they are to remain. The vines should be trained in numbers for effect. Ten or a dozen plants in a circle around a six-foot pole, with pegs and twine from the plants to the top of the pole, is soon a mass of verdure with exquisite eyes of scarlet, lovely to behold.

MEXICAN VINE.

This vine has a tuber like an Irish potato, from which it can be propagated. The leaves are broad and thick, and gracefully festooned with tassels of white flowers, which are heavily perfumed. The vine is of a rapid summer growth. Plant the tuber in the spring or fall.

MARIGOLD.

Sow the seed early in the spring. Save seed only from the earliest and largest blooms, marking by little strings tied to the stems. With even the greatest care, marigolds are liable to deteriorate. Be watchful in immediately destroying such plants as bear inferior and single blooms.

The marigold is an annual, but not hardy. It is improved by transplanting. Support the plants by tying them to stout stakes. Plant in clusters, and trim occasionally. We have seen them equal to the finest dahlia, and larger in size, of the most beautiful shades, from straw to orange.

VERBENA

Can be reared from cuttings and from seed. It flowers the same year from the seed sown in the spring. Plant in masses in a warm exposure to the sun, and enrich the soil with vegetable manure. September and October are the best months to put out cuttings in new beds.

Verbena can be made more continuous in blooming, by trimming the beds down after the blooming season is over.   They are beautiful in all varieties, but only the purple and white heliotrope are fragrant. The scarlet is the gayest.

Verbena requires change of soil every few years, and is particularly grateful for new rich earth.   The renovation should be made in the fall.   Verbena looks very handsome, grown in beds on *lawns*, being in fine contrast with the green grass.

HONEYSUCKLES.

These climbing shrubs are most of them natives.   They can be propagated by layers, suckers and cuttings.

The *English* honeysuckle is of rapid growth, and very luxuriant and fragrant. It is an evergreen.   All honeysuckles require strong, rich soil, with good depth, to sustain their vigorous growth.

Thin out honeysuckles in the fall, and divest of all superfluous shoots, and shorten in the shoots of last year. If bare at the bottom, and only flowering high up, cut down the vine to within four inches of the ground. The vines will soon send forth new shoots, which can be trained advantageously.

The *Bratton* honeysuckle is an exquisite evergreen hybrid, originated in Winnsboro', South Carolina. The leaves are a light green, smooth and pointed, overhung with feathery festoons of pale yellow flowers, shading off to white. It is the handsomest of all the honeysuckles I have seen. It is extremely difficult to propagate, and, unlike most cuttings, will only take in *rich* soil.

The *yellow* and *red woodbines* are very ornamental for pillars and porches. The graceful flowers are succeeded by bright red wax berries, which decorate the vines for months. These are readily propagated from cuttings.

JESSAMINES.

The *yellow* jessamine is native, and will live if the plants are taken from the uplands. It is evergreen, and gorgeous in flowering. The perfume is delicious. The leaf and flower are poisonous, and hence it should never be planted within the reach of children.

The *white* jessamine is an exceedingly elegant plant, delicate and fragrant, and not surpassed by any of its species. It is pure in color, and exquisite in perfume, with fringy leaves and dark green stems. It may be multiplied from suckers, but is of slow growth until fully established, when it grows rapidly.

LILAC.

The *purple* is the most common and the most desirable. The *white* is rarer and more delicate, and does not bloom as freely as the purple. It is also difficult to establish.

The *Persian* lilac is still more delicate in flowering, and very beautiful. All lilacs should have protected situations. Destroy the suckers and trim the bushes in the fall. They can be propagated by the suckers.

SNOWBALL.

A most conspicuous bush with cluster balls of tiny white flowers, like the hydrangea. It readily grows from suckers, layers or cuttings. It grows eight or ten feet high. No flower garden should be without it, for this is one of the most showy and beautiful of the deciduous shrubs.

DAHLIAS.

These can be easily propagated by division of the roots—the only method necessary for our gardens—though they can be raised from seed.

Sandy soil is best adapted to their successful cultivation. Moisture is important to their perfection in flowering. Plant the tubers early in the spring, in a light hot-bed, slightly covering them with earth, and being careful to protect from the cold. Water well until they sprout, when you may divide the root as you would potatoes for planting, leaving only one eye on each slip. The less of the old tuber planted the better.

Plant the cut tubers in March or April, in the situation designated for blooming. They increase prodigiously. Allow only one stem to each plant, and cut off the side branches, from one to three feet from

9

the ground, according to the height of the bush.

Rich loam induces luxuriant growth of leaves and imperfect flowers. Whenever dahlias are single they should be thrown away, as such will never improve.

The only remedy for the greenbug is to cautiously watch for it in the morning, and to pick it off and destroy.

Shade of every kind is injurious to dahlias. When they are constantly watered, the ground should be heavily mulched with coarse litter, the better to retain moisture, and to prevent the earth around the plant hardening. Every dahlia should have a frame, or, what is better, be tied to a stout stake, with a soft band.

BURNING BUSH.

An elegant shrub, growing eight or ten feet high. The flowers are purple, growing in clusters, succeeded by brilliant scarlet fruit, which remains until after the leaves have fallen. This shrub can be raised from seed planted in the fall, or propagated by cuttings. It should be planted in a shady and sheltered situation.

FRINGE TREE, OR WEEPING ASH,

"Daddy Greybeard," is a native, deciduous shrub, which grows twelve feet high. It is difficult to transplant, and does best when grafted on the common ash. Light loam is most congenial to this shrub.

PYRUS JAPONICA.

This is a deciduous plant, and should be transplanted in the fall. The bloom of the red is exceedingly gay in very early spring, the flowers profusely covering the bush, before the leaves appear. The blush is also very handsome. This plant throws up a great number of suckers, from which it can readily be increased. But, in multiplying by this method, there is a disadvantage in unguarded selection from suckers.

Root suckers are very troublesome in transmitting to the sucker plant the *habit* of throwing up numerous suckers, and thus generally failing to form sufficient root to 'support itself. *Offshoots,* or *stem suckers,* differ from these, and are excellent for propagation.

DEUTZIA.

This elegant deciduous shrub is a native of Japan and China. It is easy of culture, and perfectly hardy, and can be increased by cuttings and layers. In the spring the plant is covered with a profusion of white blossoms, which are highly fragrant.

The rough-leaved deutzia is used by the Japanese cabinet-makers for polishing wood. The *slender deutzia* is more airy and graceful in appearance, growing three feet high, with a slightly pendant habit. The leaves are only an inch long, and the flowers are star-shaped, of a delicate paper white. It requires a rich, light soil.

HYDRANGEA.

This is a deciduous shrub, and, being tolerably hardy, will grow in the open air where the winters are not too severe. They require shade to grow or bloom well, and when in flower need profuse watering. The pink variety is most usual, but the color can be changed to *blue* by mixing in a large portion of decayed leaves and swamp earth. If the plant is very thick, the oldest branches may be thinned out, never cuttting out any of the *young* shoots, as these bear the flowers. Propagate by offshoots or cuttings.

EVERGREENS.

These will grow in any soil, but are improved in rapidity of growth by deep digging and manuring. Be very cautious in *pruning* evergreens, because many of them are seriously injured by the knife. The *Weeping Cypress* and *Norway Spruce* we know it is detrimental to prune. Tying with twine is all that is necessary to bring them into proper shape.

In *planting* evergreens, see the directions elsewhere given for *transplanting*.

For *propagation*, see directions for raising *cuttings*, with more shading. Evergreens can be easily reared from the seed, and the plants are more symmetrical and healthy than those raised from cuttings. Seedlings should not be transplanted until they are two years old, but a better plan is to plant the seed where the trees will stand.

The *best* plan, however, is to buy good trees and plants from the nearest *nursery*.

We subjoin the names of those which we *know* to be desirable for the flower garden:

DEODAR CYPRESS.

This is commonly called *cedar*. It is a native of the Himalaya mountains, where it attains the height of one hundred and fifty feet, with a trunk thirty feet in circumference. It is the most beautiful of all resinous evergreens, and is of very rapid growth, growing in ordinary soil at least one foot a year, and in trenched ground two feet annually.

This superb tree grows well in our climate, and would be valuable timber growth for this country. Several thousand bushels of the seed were imported into England by the Government, and placed in the hands of reliable nursery-men, to cultivate, on condition of returning one-half to the Government at the end of three years, to be planted for timber growth.

The wood of the Deodar cypress is compact, resinous, highly fragrant, and of a deep, rich color, like polished brown agate. The wood of this tree, in the roofs of buildings, was found perfectly sound after more than *two hundred* years. Some used in constructing a bridge in Cashmere was but little decayed after *four hundred* years' exposure to the action of the water.

The tree is most handsome when only allowed one main trunk, from which the limbs droop in the most graceful manner.

FUNEREAL CYPRESS.

This is a beautiful, feathery, cedar-like tree, which attains the height of fifty or sixty feet. It is one of the most desirable of this kind of evergreens.

HEATH'S CYPRESS.

A fine, dark evergreen, with reddish stems and stalks. This plant will only thrive in partially shaded situations.

PYRAMIDAL CYPRESS,

Is very handsome, and naturally assumes the pyramidal form, growing to the height of twenty feet. The cypress tribe may all be propagated by layers and cuttings, but much more readily by seeds. These generally lie in the ground a year before they sprout.

NORWAY SPRUCE.

This is a hardy and ornamental evergreen, of yellowish green foliage. It is the tallest of the European firs, with a straight, slender trunk, thick foliage and drooping branches. Although formal in appearance, when young, it is one of the most ornamental of all evergreens when grown, when the limbs droop in depending curves, adding fresh graces to it.

The *Norway Spruce* will thrive in any soil and adapts itself to any situation. It should not be pruned at all. It attains the height of one hundred feet.

CHILI PINE.

A beautiful tree, when healthy, which it rarely is. It attains, in its native soil, one hundred feet in height. It is elegant and unique.

CALIFORNIA ARBOR VITÆ.

A very handsome specimen, with fans turned in diverse directions. The stems and stalks are red. It is of rapid growth, and attains the height of fifty feet.

GOLDEN ARBOR VITÆ.

This Chinese variety of the arbor vitæ is the choicest of its kind. It should never be pruned.   It grows only six feet high, and is perfectly symmetrical, and very compact in foliage.   It is almost golden hued in color, which gives it the name it bears.   In winter, however, it changes to a rusty color.   But its symmetry and usual beauty is sufficient amends for a temporary discoloration.

PYRAMIDAL ARBOR VITÆ.

This is also a compact growth, the color bright green, and grows ten feet high.   It should never be pruned.

PALM-LEAF ARBOR VITÆ,

Has large, beautiful fans, in graceful foliage.

HEMLOCK SPRUCE.

This elegant tree is of a lively, green color.   Humid soil is best adapted to its culture.   It is rather difficult to transplant.

This spruce is not of such monotonous formality as the Norway spruce, the limbs being still more depending.

The hemlock is considered the most beautiful tree of this family. It is of slow growth until fully established. It has great softness and delicacy of foliage, and slender, tapering branches. It bears severe pruning without the slightest injury.

CEDAR OF LEBANON.

This magnificent tree will grow in any soil. It advances with great rapidity in growth, but can scarcely equal the lovely, silvery *Deodar*. The cones of the Lebanon cedar are four inches long, and beautifully drawn. Deep trenching is of amazing utility in advancing the growth of this evergreen.

JAPAN CEDAR.

This cedar attains the height of one hundred feet, and is very ornamental.

SILVER FIR.

Planted favorably, no tree is of more rapid growth than this. In a dry, compact soil, it grows slowly and is short lived, but in deep, rich loam, and a sheltered position, it will grow rapidly, and with great vigor.

The *California Silver Fir* is a trim and beautiful tree, which grows two hundred feet high, branching out from near the ground, and preserving a conic symmetry, with the utmost precision, creating an impression that it must have been trimmed by an experienced gardener. This tree, when first introduced into Europe, brought *sixteen dollars* for seedlings of one year.

10

JUNIPERS.

These evergreens display a silvery green foliage, growing in pyramidal form naturally. The leaves are small. Plants can be raised from the seed, which require eighteen months to vegetate. A dry loam on gravelly sub-soil is best adapted to their culture.

Junipers should be encouraged to throw off branches from the ground, if intended for ornamental trees. Pruning the lower branches spoils the beauty of the trees, which are naturally perfectly plume-like in shape.

BALSAM FIR.

When planted in good soil, in a few years this fir becomes a perfect pyramid of dark green foliage. Rich, sandy soil is best adapted to it. It is hardy, easily trans-planted, and grows rapidly and with great vigor. The greatest objection to the balsam fir is its early decay. It is short-lived, and becomes very ragged in its appearance when it attains its full growth.

HOLLY.

We have a fine native species, which is of slow growth, but is lovely even as a shrub. It is extremely difficult to transplant and establish. The best time to remove the plants from the woods is just before the buds begin to shoot. The smaller the plant the better the success of transplanting. Protect them a long time from the sun's rays.

The native holly grows from twenty to forty feet high, and if not trimmed the lower limbs rest upon the ground, and the whole tree forms a beautiful symmetrical cone. In the fall it is covered with red berry fruit, which remain all winter.

HOLLY-LEAVED BERBERRY.

This is not so beautiful as our native holly, but is easier to transplant. It grows six feet high.

TEA PLANT.

This plant is a half-hardy evergreen shrub, thickly branched, with dark green foliage, like the camelia japonica. The bloom is white. It grows from four to six feet high, when cultivated for tea-making, but will attain a height of ten feet when not dwarfed by this process.

A light yellowish loam, well mixed with sand and moderately moist, is best for this plant. Earth mould, or any vegetable manure, will increase its vigor. In order to make it assume a round and bushy outline, the ends of the shoots should be pinched off with the fingers, (this plant must not be touched with the knife,) otherwise it will grow too straggling.

This shrub may be propagated from seed or cuttings. The seed should be planted two or three inches deep, and will vegetate in two or three months. The cuttings must be planted in October, and taken from matured shoots. The seedlings or cuttings can be transplanted when a year old.

LAUREL.

All the *laurels* are fine, either the native species or the English. The *kalmia*, or native laurel, should be cut down to the ground, in transplanting, to do well, being an exception to its species in this respect.

The *English* laurel is one of our most beautiful evergreens, with large, shining, green leaves. It grows twenty feet high, and bears a small white flower. It is of very rapid growth, and a desirable tree in the flower yard.

CAPE JESSAMINE.

This handsome evergreen has beautiful dark green leaves, with a rich camelia-like flower, of delicious fragrance. It grows ten feet high, and may be propagated by layers or cuttings. They can also be grown in water, in glass, until rootlets appear, and the glass then filled up with sand. When established in the sand, break off the glass and set in the ground without disturbing the roots. Plant *cuttings* in sand, and keep saturated with water, and they will be sure to succeed. The cape jessamine is handsome in single plants or hedges. In either case they should be allowed to stool.

CAMELIA JAPONICA.

This splendid evergreen can be grown out of doors in the more southern localities of this State, and therefore a description of its cultivation will not be out of place in this treatise. The camelia can be increased by layers, cuttings and seed.

Layers can be made from shoots of the last year's growth. Trim the shoot clear of all side shoots or leaves as far as necessary to bed them. Dig the earth carefully, breaking it fine and mixing rich earth-mould with it, and let it be slightly raised above the level of the ground, or if the branch be too high from the ground, place a pot filled with earth under the branch. Make a slanting cut upwards half through the branch, immediately below and close to a bud, which is termed "*tongueing*" it. Cut off the tip end of the tongue. This cut should be made at such a distance as to permit its being bent down into the ground. Give the branch a slightly twisting motion in the process, to prevent snapping it off and to open it; then pin it down to the ground with a forked stick. Cover with two or three inches of earth. Then press the earth gently on and around the layer, and shorten to one or two buds above the surface. This description of *layering* applies generally to all plants that admit of this method of propagation. Layering may be done on the last year's growth just before the sap begins to rise in the spring; or, on the the new growth of the year, any time from the middle of June to the end of July, and even later. If pots are used for this operation, the earth in the pot must be kept very moist until the layer has rooted, care being taken in watering not to wash away the earth from around the cut.

Plants propagated by *seed* are so symmetrical and healthy that they will amply repay the pains necessary to be taken to raise them by this method. Select a plant to bear seed, the *pistils* of whose blooms are perfect. If you have none, you need not attempt the experiment. Then take a fine camel-hair pencil and put it gently on the *pollen* of the bloom of another plant (always a *double* variety), then, with this on the pencil, dust it lightly on the *stigma* of the bloom you have selected to bear seed, just as it is newly expanded. Between the hours of ten and twelve in the forenoon is the most proper time for the operation. The seed must be sown as soon as ripe. Plant them about an inch deep, in pots filled with leaf mould, loam and white sand, in equal portions, and place the pots in a warm situation. When six inches high transfer from the pots to the places where you desire them to grow. These will bloom the second year. Endless varieties can be produced by this method of *hybridizing*, which can successfully be applied to the rose and many other flowers.

For the cultivation of the camelia the soil should be enriched to the depth of two feet with vegetable mould. *Animal* manure must never be applied to the japonica. In watering, be careful never to let any water fall on the blooms, as this causes premature decay and fading of the colors.

When the plant is young, during the heat of summer, mulch well around the stem; and, if the plant be vigorous, water freely during dry weather; but if the plant be sickly, shade with evergreen boughs and water often, but sparingly. The japonica, out of doors, attains a height of from ten to twenty-five feet.

PITTOSPORUM.

This evergreen is a native of China, and quite hardy with us, growing to a height of fifteen feet. The foliage is very handsome, and is dark green. It bears clusters of small white flowers, of fine fragrance. There is also a variegated variety of the pittosporum. This ornamental evergreen will grow with the most simple treatment. It is easily propagated by cuttings.

TWISTED CYPRESS.

This is a desirable evergreen, growing fifteen feet high. Its foliage partakes of the appearance of both cedar and arbor vitæ, and seems to have a tendency to twist; hence its name. It forms a beautiful conical tree.

OLEANDER.

This is a beautiful, erect-growing shrub, of easy culture. It is subject to disease from becoming infested with a white, scaly insect, which must be destroyed by washing. The single is not so handsome as the double rose, which is exceedingly tender. Oleanders grow eight feet high. When they become sluggish, and do not bloom well, they should be cut down to the ground. They require some protection in the winter. The roots have wonderful vitality. Indeed, many evergreens have the same quality, and often, when apparently dead for a year, will suddenly put forth new and vigorous. We have known an oleander root longer than this in a dormant condition, and to send forth fine healthy shoots.

CORK OAK.

This is a handsome evergreen, imported by the Government from Spain, and is suitable for a *shade tree*. The leaves are shaped like the holly, but rounder and of a paler green, similar to the live oak, with very large acorns. It is of very rapid growth, having grown two feet the first year. It is said to make a noble tree in less than twelve years.

It is rather difficult to transplant, but with shade and extra care in moving, not many will fail, although all lose the foliage, and renew on their recovery from the removal. The propagation is very easy from the acorns.

FLORIDA MAGNOLIA.

This magnificent and noble tree is indigenous to our Southern States. Inland it attains a height of from ten to twenty feet. Nearer the coast it is of gigantic growth. There is not a more magnificent sight in the world than an avenue of these superb evergreens, with their monstrous blooms, such as grow in the lower parts of South Carolina and Georgia.

The *magnolia* is of slow growth, but always elegant and symmetrical. The health and vigor of the trees are promoted by occasionally giving a top-dressing of salt, not allowing the salt to come in contact with the trunk or roots of the tree.

CHINESE MAGNOLIA.

This is a much more hardy species, and soon attains its full height, of six or eight feet. The flowers are lily-shaped, smaller than the Florida, and of two colors, the

11

white and the purple. When full grown it loses its lower branches, and assumes the appearance of an immense umbrella.

EUONYMOUS.

The foliage is a deep, shining green, of rapid growth, and suitable for hedges. The single plants require close and frequent pruning. The silver-edged is much the handsomer. It grows well from cuttings. No necessity for small plants to have roots, as they will grow without. Height, ten to fifteen feet. Seedlings change very much in character from the parent plant.

MESPILUS JAPONICA.

This is a fine plant with large leaves, white underneath. It bears small white flowers on a spike, which produces, in a favorable climate, fruit of the size of a walnut, of a fine yellow blush color. It is of easy culture, and perfectly hardy.

PRIVET.

The *privets* are all handsome in hedges. The *American* bears a black berry, and the *English* a green berry, and both make good hedges. We also have the silver-edged, with variegated foliage. The Japan privet has long, oval leaves, of a bright green color, and is perfectly hardy. The *L. Lucida* privet has elegant, thick, camelia-like foliage, and grows from ten to fifteen feet high, into a handsome and symmetrical tree. It bears spikes of small white flowers, succeeded by black berries, which hang on all winter.

TREE BOX.

This makes an ornamental hedge, and grows very rapidly. It is suitable for face hedging to other growth, to hide defects, growing well under trees. In single plants it grows twenty feet high, and can be trimmed into any shape desired. The gol-den-edged is a very pretty variety.

The *dwarf* box is best for edging beds, and should first be cultivated from cut-tings, in plantations, and well rooted before bordering, because so uncertain.

Box edgings which have remained a number of years in the same place, should be taken up and relaid. Dig them up and cut off the lower roots with a hatchet, and square the young top shoots with a sharp knife. The surplus box can be used in other parts of the garden.

FRENCH FURZE.

An erect, prickly, evergreen shrub. It makes handsome and impenetrable hedges. It must be closely and regularly trimmed, or it becomes unsightly. Old and scragly grown trees should be cut down to the ground, and they will soon put out again. It grows four feet high. It should be more cultivated, for it is very gay and beautiful in bloom. It blossoms early in the spring, in flowers of pea-bloom shape. In fact, it is more or less in bloom all the year; hence the old French proverb, that "love goes out of fashion when the furze goes out of bloom."

WILD ORANGE,

Elsewhere known as the Carolina cherry, is one of the most beautiful vegetable productions of the South. The foliage is a dark, shining green, handsome at all seasons. It has a small white bloom, succeeded by black fruit in berries. Its growth is extraordinarily vigorous and rapid. It is universally used in hedges; and forms, when trimmed, solid walls of verdure, from ten to twenty feet high. The hedges require trimming twice in the year, in spring, and in fall after it has completed its growth for

the season.   Single trees can be trimmed
into any shape desired.

The seed are difficult to germinate, and
when planted sometimes lie dormant in the
ground *two* years before they come up.   But
by the following plan they can be easily
raised.   Put the seed, when ripe, into some
vessel, with plenty of fresh ashes or lime
mixed through them.   In a week or ten days
the hulls will readily rub off with the hands.
Having hulled the seed, soak them in water
until some of them burst, then plant immediately, in a rich bed.   The first soaking
rain will bring them up like peas.   Transplant when one year old, when in a dormant state; though the better plan is to
sow the seed where they are to stand.   The
proper time to sow seed is in February or
March.

WHITE PINE.

This is the loftiest pine in the Atlantic States, attaining a height of two hundred feet. The cones are four or five inches long. Young trees make an elegant appearance, owing to the lightness and delicacy of the foliage. It is not easily grown at the South. It is precarious of life, and when transplanted is liable to die. Hence we say that this is an *undesirable* evergreen.

OLIVE.

Olives require a temperate and equable climate. Too great heat is as hurtful to them as severe cold. Sudden changes of temperature are exceedingly injurious; hence it would seem to be little adapted to our variable climate.

It is very delicate, and difficult to establish in our latitude. If planted at all, it should have the benefit of a shady situation. The climate of Florida, however, suits

the olive, and in East Florida are several
large olive trees planted by a colony of
Greeks in 1783.   There is a native olive
found thinly disseminated through Florida
and along the shores of the Gulf of Mexico,
as far as Louisiana, sometimes known as
the *Devil-wood*.

A humid soil or situation is injurious to
the olive.   It will grow from cuttings and
pieces of root, and is very tenacious of life.

The old proverb, that "no man who has
planted an olive has ever tasted of its fruit,"
though not literally true, has arisen from
the extreme slowness of its growth.

The *fragrant olive* is a native of China
and Japan, and is a more interesting plant.
The flowers are white, growing in bunches,
and highly fragrant, and are used by the
Chinese for perfuming their teas.   This species requires the same treatment as the European olive, and is of very slow growth.

YEWS.

These evergreens belong to the pine genus. The foliage resembles the hemlock spruce, but the fruit is not a cone, but a small red berry, in the hollow part of the extremity of which a small green seed appears. The yew can be clipped, without injury, into any shape. The leaves of the yew are very poisonous, both to men and cattle. The yews are all of extremely slow growth, and therefore *very undesirable* in the flower garden.

The English yew grows to the height of twenty feet, and the Irish variety ten feet. The Canadian yew is a low, prostrate shrub, entirely worthless.

WASHINGTONIA GIGANTEA.

This is the giant pine of California. Doubtless its mammoth dimensions may be attributed to the richness of the soil in which it grows. The whole number of these trees in existence, young and old, does not exceed five hundred, and all are comprised within an area of about fifty acres. This spot is a rich gold region near Sonora.

One of these noble trees was, by some *gigantic* accident, overthrown, some forty or fifty years since, the trunk of which was three hundred feet in length and the tree had, undoubtedly, attained the height of five hundred feet, when standing alive. At the butt it was one hundred and ten feet in circumference, or about thirty-six feet in diameter. On the bark quite a soil had accumulated, on which large shrubs were growing, elevated twenty-two feet above the ground. The seed of this tree has been calculated to have germinated when Moses was a baby.

The leaves are triangular and scale-like, as in the cedar, and the wood is a deep red. The cones require two years to attain their full growth, when they are up-wards of a foot in length and nearly four inches in diameter.

The growth of this giant pine is very slow, and its appearance, while young, not striking. It will attain a proper height for a flower garden in *fifty* years, and its full height in about *one thousand* years.

AUCUBAN JAPONICA,

Or Blotch plant, is of slow and preca-rious growth, and only attains an incon-siderable height. It has yellow spotted or blotched leaves, hence its name. The flowers are small and insignificant. If planted at all, it requires a shady situation to grow more freely. The hot sun is fatal to the Aucuban japonica.

LAWNS.

To succeed well with lawns, the ground must be *trenched*, that the grass roots may penetrate at least two feet deep, and not be injured by drought, and preserve the freshness of color throughout the summer.

After the ground has been trenched, it must be smoothly raked, and allowed to settle a week or ten days before planting. Loosen the surface with the rake when ready to sow the seed. Grass seed should be sown heavily, to cover the ground completely. After sowing, the ground should be rolled with a heavy roller.

Lawns should be frequently mown, and rolled after every rain, to make them velvety and close in texture. It is of great importance to have the plats heavily seeded, for then weeds can have no chance to grow. Never allow the grass to go to seed, but regularly mow every three or four weeks, from April to October. Never permit the grass to grow higher than four inches.

In very dry weather, all lawns should be watered. In small plats, where a thick turf is required, the quantity of seed must be doubled.

A mixture of grass seed is better than any single variety alone. For instance, sow equal parts of *red-top* and *blue-grass*— the *Hungarian* and *Palmer* grass, etc.

The time for sowing lawns is in the spring or autumn. Sow broadcast, and as uniformly as possible, slightly covering the seed with a sprinkling of vegetable earth, and roll it well. With constant care a lawn will last a long time, but if abandoned to itself, it will have to be renewed every few years. Lawns require to be weeded every spring and fall. They should be top-dressed in autumn with long ma-

12

nure, raking off the straw in the spring, before the grass begins to grow. A mixture of guano and soot is equally good for a top dressing. A sprinkling of vegetable earth is the best fertilizer that can be applied to a strong soil. This should be done once in three years.

Small lawns are improved by resowing every year, to keep them fresh and thick. If old lawns become mossy, the best plan is to harrow with an iron rake, and instead of disturbing the grass it will improve it. Guano, mixed half-and-half with sand or charcoal, is a great renovator of grass plats, if sown before a rain in February. By neglecting to mow grass too long, the roots become tender, and die under the heat of the sun.

INDEX.

136   INDEX.

PUBLICATIONS

O F

P. B. GLASS,

(SUCCESSOR TO R. L. BRYAN,)

PUBLISHER, BOOKSELLER AND STATIONER,

175 Richardson Street,

COLUMBIA, S. C.

LIST OF BOOKS

PUBLISHED BY

P. B. GLASS, (Successor to R. L. Bryan,)

COLUMBIA, SOUTH CAROLINA.

BARNWELL·

Manual of Supplementary References to the Course of Lectures upon Moral Philosophy, delivered before the Junior Class of the S. C. College, by Rev. R. W. BARNWELL.

LaBORDE.

History of the South Carolina College by Dr. M. LaBORDE.

LIEBER·

The Character of the Gentleman, by Dr. FRANCIS LIEBER.

RION.

Ladies' Southern Florist, by Mrs. JAMES H. RION.

THOMAS.

The Carolina Tribute to Calhoun, edited by Prof. J. P. THOMAS.

WILLIAMS.

Treatise on Plane and Spherical Trigonometry, by Prof. M. J. WILLIAMS.

DESCRIPTIVE CATALOGUE

OF

BOOKS PUBLISHED BY P. B. GLASS,

(SUCCESSOR TO R. L. BRYAN,)

Columbia, S. C.

History of the South Carolina College,

From its incorporation, December 19, 1801, to November 25, 1857. Including Sketches of its
Presidents and Professors. With an Appen-
dix containing a brief history of the Soci-
eties of the College, a complete list of the
Trustees, Presidents, Professors, Tutors, Treas-
urers, Librarians, and Alumni—from 1801 to
1858—as well as a record of the honors awarded
from the period of the first commencement to the
commencement of 1858, inclusive. By MAXA-
MILLIAN LABORDE, M. D., Professor of Metaphysics, Logic, and Rhetoric, South Carolina
College. 1 vol., 8vo. Price, muslin, $2; half
calf, $3.50.

Extract from the Author's Preface.

* * * * "I have endeavored to trace it from
its beginning to a very recent period; to give the
story of its trials, its reverses, and its triumphs.
Nothing important to the truth of history has been
suppressed. I might have sketched a more beautiful
and attractive picture, which would have been looked
upon with a higher pride and admiration. * * *

It would not have been the history of the College, and truth would have been sacrificed to taste and sentiment. But the College will not suffer by such an exposure. * * * * No feeling of modesty shall constrain me from saying, that from the first day of its existence to the present moment, no body of young men assembled for a similar purpose in any of the Institutions of the country, have been freer from irregularities, exhibited a higher honor and a nobler virtue, reflected more credit upon the Alma Mater, and vindicated more clearly in future life their claim to the respect and confidence of the public.

OPINIONS OF THE PRESS.

From the Winnsboro' Register, Mr. DAVIDSON, *Contributing Editor.*

"It claims to be—and very thoroughly and faithfully is—a History of the South Carolina College. Our friends are aware that we expected much at the hands of the biographer of our mental mother—him at whose feet we sat in the days agone. High as were these expectations, they have been fully met in the volume before us. The spirit is genial and appreciative. The work we consider an admirable contribution to the history of education, an important section in the History of South Carolina, and a valuable contribution to the bibliographical literature of the State."

From The Courant.

"Dr. LaBorde's style is singularly chaste, while he yet avoids the fault of dryness, but no glow of imagination, or flush of fancy, can betray him into meretricious ornament, or the *splendida vitia* of even some of our best writers. * * * The mere matter of collecting facts, marshalling dates, putting down numbers and arranging names, is not the object of this volume. Upon these dry bones he has breathed a living spirit, and the History of the College passes before us, on these pages, like some splendid panorama. We shall not say that the dead seem alive again, but that we see them in the most perfect representation; standing out in vivid columns like some of the best word-painting of Livy or Lord Macaulay."

From the Cheraw Gazette.

"If Professor LaBorde was never to write another paragraph, this clothing of a comparatively barren and sterile subject in a foliage rich in the variety of its beautiful and fascinating tints, would establish his reputation as an author, as a historian, and as a scholar, high up in the niche of the eminent."

From the Laurensville Herald.

"The author has placed all favorers of education in the State, and especially the alumni of the College, under great obligations, for the manner in which he has touched off the various struggles and trials of the College. This book is of interest to all."

From the Chester Standard.

"It is written in a pleasant and entertaining style, and will be enjoyed by thousands of eager admirers."

From the Anderson Gazette.

"The History is faithfully traced. It is a book that every one will find something of interest in."

From the Greenville Mountaineer.

"Dr. LaBorde has given to the public not only a historical volume, but a very interesting book, one that will command the attention of even those who never knew of the existence of the College, while for those whose memories are linked with the institution, he has contributed a work of lasting interest."

From the Greenville Mountaineer, contributed by B. F. PERRY.

"The South Carolina College and the State of South Carolina are under great obligations to Dr. LaBorde for his labors and success in tracing, from its foundation up to the present time, the history of this noble institution, and sketching, in such graphic terms, its Presidents and Professors. These portraitures of character are worthy of the pen of Plutarch. How beautifully it gives the high and commanding character of the eloquent and gifted MAXCY, the first and most revered President of the Col-

lege. How truthfully is told the life and character of the learned
utilitarian infidel, COOPER. * * * The sketch of BARNWELL
is that of an accomplished scholar, statesman, patriot, gentleman
and Christian.   The character of the brilliant, eloquent, generous
PRESTON, is drawn in terms which would do credit to the finest
sketches of Macaulay. The pure, virtuous and learned HENRY, is
described with feelings which go to the heart of the reader, and
produce an admiration and sympathy for the man.   The analysis
of the learning, character and mind of the wonderful THORNWELL,
displays surpassing ability as a writer and scholar. A just tribute
is well paid to the character of Dr. LIEBER, whose mind, stored
with all learning, ancient and modern, has given himself a world-
wide fame.   The character of Bishop ELLIOT is well drawn, noble
in person, noble in intellect, noble in every Christian virtue.   The
sketch of the deeply lamented NOTT is a lovely one.   There are
many drawn with equal truth and beauty, who honored the College as Professors, and who are now honored by the charming
historian."

From the Spartanburg Express.

"In giving this work to the public, Dr. LaBorde has not only
added to his own reputation as a scholar and writer, but he has made
a most valuable contribution to the literature of his native State.
The composition of this book seems to have been to him a labor
of love, and we think we are not mistaken in saying that upon
no one could the task have been more appropriately devolved."

From the Darlington Flag.

"To the alumni of the College, to whom this work is dedicated,
it will be invaluable, while the great fund of information it contains, the pure and graceful style in which it is written, and the
deep interest which the public has always manifested, in every-
thing connected with the institution, and the past history which it
records, will secure it a hearty welcome from the general reader."

From the Pee Dee Times.

"Every alumnus of our noble old State College, every student,
every friend of education in the State, will thank Dr. LaBorde
for writing a truthful, most reliable, and very interesting history
of the institution which, for more than fifty years, has been an
honor and blessing to South Carolina, * * * This history
should be in the library of every reading man who loves his
native land and her institutions."

From the Abbeville Banner.

" To recall to mind, as the author has done, the scenes which make up the grand college drama, having a run of fifty years, with the entire State as an audience, must have been a pleasant task to the author, and we may venture the opinion that his labors will be duly appreciated by the reading public."

From Southern Presbyterian Review, Dr. GEO. HOWE, *Editor.*

"Dr. LaBorde has performed a very acceptable service to the people of this State, to the friends of education and to the numerous alumni of the South Carolina College—by the historical work whose title is given above. Rarely have we ever read a work of this character with greater zest. Partly, it may be owing to the value we set upon this cherished institution, which has accomplished so much for the State, partly to our acquaintance with the man who, for the last thirty years, has been numbered among its instructors, and partly to the decided relish we profess to have for compositions of this kind. Much honor is due to the skill and judgment of the historian himself, and the easy and lively style in which his work is written. There is enough of history to enable us to follow the thread of events both as to the external and interior state of the College, without that multiplicity of detail which would weary and disgust. We are now amused with the pranks of the students, now sympathise with the troubles in which the government of the College is involved, and are always interested in the biographical sketches, and the analysis of character, which Dr. LaBorde has given of the several Professors and Presidents, who have either been removed by death or have resigned the chairs they occupied for other pursuits. Some of them passed away with the last generation, and are only remembered by the few aged men who yet survive. Others were our cotemporaries, and some of these are yet among us. So with the histories of living men, or those just now departed, and gone forth to the public, an estimate of their labors, and an analysis of their character, was a matter at once delicate and difficult of execution. Dr. LaBorde, conscious of the goodness of his intentions, has gone forward boldly, and has striven to hold the balances with an impartial hand."

From DeBow's Review.

" Here is a work which will be prized by the numerous alumni of the old South Carolina College, as by scholars throughout the South. It is from the pen of the Professor of Metaphysics, Logic and Rhetoric, and includes the whole period of the exis-

13

tence of the College from 1801 to date, giving an account of the range of its studies, the lives of the Presidents, Professors and more distinguished students, with catalogues of all the graduating classes, &c. Dr. LaBorde has accomplished his task with much ability, and we could wish to see as much done for our other institutions of learning."

From Russell's Magazine, (Contributed.)

"When a motion was made, in the Board of Trustees, that the archives of the South Carolina College be placed at the disposal of Dr. LaBorde, to facilitate his writing a history of the institution, we thought that the *right thing* was about to be done by the *right man*. The occasional mention of the forthcoming volume, in the columns of the Columbia press, and the significant hints of the various gentlemen who stood in the confidential relation of Macenas to the author, inspired us with fresh confidence, and we were, therefore, not at all surprised at the **high** commendation and universal applause, which has attended the consummation of so worthy a book in so able a manner. When the press has spoken at all it has spoken in terms of enthusiastic praise, and from all parts of the State we have seen notices of it of the most laudatory kind, under initials or pseudonymic, in which it was easy to detect those well able and qualified to judge of its merits, and whose information is a passport to fame. The author of the portraits of Nott, and Preston, and Henry, has been compared to Plutarch. His style is thought, in places, not inferior to Macaulay, and his weird power of word-painting to rival that master of pictured prose, the immortal Livy. This is great praise. To put one in mind of the most elegant writers of Greece, Rome and Great Britain, is a compliment which should compensate an American writer for all the discouragements to which he is doomed in the path of literature, and impose upon him with the exhibition of a just pride, the observance of a chastened humility. We regard it, then, as an approved verdict, that the History of the South Carolina College has done infinite credit to its author, conferred a lasting service upon the College, and added new lustre to the literature of the South.

LaBorde's History of the South Carolina College will be sent by Mail, to any part of the United States, on the receipt of two dollars and thirty cents. Address P. B. GLASS, Publisher, Columbia, S. C.

The Carolina Tribute to Calhoun,

Edited by Prof. JOHN P. THOMAS, (of the State
Military Academy of South Carolina.) With
a superb Portrait, on steel, of John C. Calhoun,
and *fac simile* autograph. One handsome 8vo.
volume, 416 pp., clo., emb., Price, $2.00.

Extract from Editor's Preface.

The present volume is commended to the people of
South Carolina with every confidence that it will be
accepted by them as a valued memento of the sad but
cherished past. Designed mainly to commemorate the
death of Calhoun, it embraces all the important inci-
dents, ceremonies and testimonials, connected with
that great event; together with the several discourses,
addresses and orations, elicited from the full hearts of
admiring Carolinians. The death at Washington;
the meeting in the Senate Hall; the removal home of
the mortal remains; the imposing demonstration at
Charleston; the Cemetery of St. Philip's; the plain
marble slab with its brief though expressive inscrip-
tion; and then the solemn gathering of our people in
various quarters—*these* are the scenes which the volume depicts—these the recollections it revives. It
thus speaks forcibly to the heart—and, moreover,
presents a record of mingled love, admiration and
grief, such, we conceive, as has been vouchsafed to but
very few men.

Herein are contained the remarks in Congress of
distinguished Senators and Representatives; the Ser-
mon of the Chaplain of the Senate; the Report of the
Committee of Twenty-five; the Narrative of the Fune-
ral Honors at Charleston; the Message of Governor
Seabrook; the Discourses of the Rev. Messrs. Barnwell, Thornwell, Miles, Palmer and Smith; and the

Orations—instinct with thought and feeling—of
Messrs. Allston, Coit, Henry, Whyte, Porcher, Ham-
mond, Rhett and Porter. Nor must we omit to refer
to the resolutions of the Pennsylvania and New York
Legislatures, the proceedings of the New York Historical Society, and to other memorials of rare interest;
all bearing the highest testimony to the virtues and
the services of our great statesman, and showing how
well the splendor of his public conduct accorded with
the stainless purity of his private life.

Precious, therefore, are the memories which this
volume embalms; useful is the lesson it teaches; and
deathless the spirit it excites. Filled with thoughts
of high import—with the sentiments **both** of laymen
and divines, its pages wear the chaste impress of
truth, and glow with the fire of genuine eloquence.
Impressively they tell of patriotism and noble self-
devotion; of duty and its stern behests; of greatness
and its large rewards; of *laurels won and cypress
scattered.*

COMMENDATIONS OF THE PRESS.

From Russell's Magazine.

"Prof. Thomas has done an essential service to the State, and
incidentally to history itself, in the compilation of this valuable
work."

From the Darlington Family Friend.

"It is a worthy tribute to the memory of the great Carolinian;
it should be found in the possession of every son of our State,
and be treasured by each as a priceless memorial of the immortal
statesman."

From the Camden Journal.

"It is a genuine tribute to exalted talent and great moral and
political worth."

From the Charleston Evening News.

" It abounds in gems, speeches and orations, and contains a large body of historical and political matter, with which Mr. Calhoun had connection in his great and eventful life."

From the Charleston Mercury.

" We heartily thank the editor for his valuable labors in making this collection."

From the Yorkville Enquirer.

" It is entirely a Southern work, Southern production and Southern sentiment, and should adorn the library of every true Southron."

From the Charleston Courier.

" The editor has given to the public a volume of 416 pages, of closely printed matter, gathering, as it were, the scattered blocks, hewn out and polished by the various artists, and piling with them a noble literary and moral monument, to the memory and virtues of the great and glorious dead."

From the Abbeville Independent Press.

" The editor, as he states in his preface, has not aspired to authorship, but has contented himself with merely arranging in a fitting casket the choice gems of others, and he has executed his task with great taste and judgment. He has erected a monument more enduring than the sculptured marble or monumental pile, and which will more effectually embalm the life, the character, the genius and public services of the great Calhoun, in the grateful memory of his admiring countrymen.

" Apart from its intrinsic merits, the work should be in the hands of every Carolinian, as an enduring record of the man whom we all delight to honor; and particularly should it be prized by the citizens of the district which gave him birth, where his memory is most cherished, and where his genius, character and public services have ever received a due appreciation."

The Carolina Tribute to Calhoun will be sent by Mail, to any part of the United States, on receipt of two dollars and thirty cents. Address P. B. GLASS, Publisher, Columbia, S. C.

A History of Upper South Carolina.

By JOHN H. LOGAN, A. M. In which is presented a lively narrative of events, in connection with many Living Names and Present Scenes, from the period of its being first penetrated by the White Man to the close of the War of Independence. Two vols., 12mo., 600 pp.,   -   - $3.00

The Character of the Gentleman.

An Address to the Students of Miami University, Ohio, on the evening before Commencement Day, in August, 1846. By FRANCIS LIEBER, LL. D., Prof. of History, Columbia College, New York; late Prof. of Political Philosophy and Economy in South Carolina College. Second and enlarged edition, 12mo. Cloth, 75 cents; paper 50 cents.

A Manual of Supplementary References

To the Course of Lectures upon Moral Philosophy, delivered before the Junior Class of the South Carolina College, by Rev. ROBERT W. BARNWELL, Prof. of Moral Philosophy, Sacred Literature, and Evidences of Christianity. 8vo., half-mor.,   -   -   -   -   -   - $1.75

Williams' Trigonometry.

Elements of Plane and Spherical Trigonometry, prepared for Schools and Colleges. By Prof. MAT. J. WILLIAMS, late of the South Carolina College. 12mo., sheep.,   -   -   -   -   -   75

P. B. GLASS,

IS SOLE AGENT OF THE STATE OF SOUTH CAROLINA

FOR THE SALE OF THE FOLLOWING BOOKS:

The Statutes of South Carolina. Twelve volumes, octavo.
Carroll's Historical Collections of South Carolina. Two volumes, octavo.
Pressley's Law of Magistrates. One volume, octavo.

—ALSO,—

Is Agent for the sale of the following Books, published in South Carolina :

The Law and Equity Reports of South Carolina.
Rivers' History of South Carolina. One volume, 8vo.; $2.
Carroll's Catechism of United States History. 12mo., cloth; 75 cents.
The Hireling and the Slave, Chicora, and other Poems; by Wm. J. Grayson. One volume, 12mo., cloth; $1.
Connor's Law Digest, $8; interleaved, $10.
Connor's Equity Digest, $12; interleaved, 2 vols., $15.
Connor's Suit at Law, $1.
Flagg's Digest, $4; interleaved, $5.
Miller's Compilation, $3.
The Country; by Wm. J. Grayson. Cloth, 50 cts.; gilt, 75 cts.
Historical Collections of the South Carolina Historical Society. Two volumes. 8vo., cloth; $5 per volume.
Gibbes' Documentary History of South Carolina. 3 vols., 8vo., cloth; $4.50.
Ramsay's History of South Carolina. 1 vol., 8vo.; $3.50.
Lieber's Reports of the Geological Survey of South Carolina; with numerous Geognostic Maps, &c. Vols. 1, 2, 3 and 4; $2.
Evans' Road Law of South Carolina.
Analysis of Butler's Analogy, Part First; by Rev. James H. Thornwell, D. D.
Review of Paley's Moral Philosophy; by same author.
Furman's Poems. 1 vol., 12mo., $1.
Johnson & Walker's Map of South Carolina; handsomely colored and mounted on rollers.
Judge O'Neall's Bench and Bar of South Carolina. 2 volumes, 8vo.; $5.

P. B. GLASS,

(SUCCESSOR TO R. L. BRYAN.,)

PUBLISHER,

BOOKSELLER AND STATIONER,

COLUMBIA, S. C.

Continues the Book Business at the Old Stand in Columbia, (for over thirty years occupied as a Bookstore,) near the Court House, and offers to the public a most complete and carefully selected stock in every department of his business.

Law, Medical, School, Theological, and

Miscellaneous Books,

GIFT BOOKS, ALBUMS, JUVENILE BOOKS.

BLANK BOOKS
Of every variety manufactured.

BIBLES
Of every variety and style of binding.

PRAYER BOOKS AND HYMN BOOKS,
For all denominations.

Music Books, Memorandum and Pass Books, Pocket Books, Invoice and Letter Books, Receipt Books, Note Books, Check Books, Bill Books, all printed, affording every facility in the Counting Room.

CONSTANTLY ON HAND

A SUPERIOR STOCK OF

STATIONERY,

Comprising Letter, Cap and Note Papers, of all sizes, qualities and descriptions; Envelope and Wrapping Papers; also Flat papers of all sizes, and is prepared to manufacture BLANK BOOKS to any pattern, at short notice. Envelopes in numberless variety and of the best quality. He has also procured a STAMPING MACHINE, and is prepared to stamp any name or seal upon paper or envelopes. Wedding Cards and Envelopes furnished, engraved, printed or written to order.

Artists, Architects and Draughtsmen will find a complete stock of materials for their use. Drawing Paper in sheets and rolls; Bristol Boards, Pastel Paper and Boards, all colors, Sketching Blocks and Books, Oil Canvas, Oil Paper, Mathematical Instruments, Pencils, Scales, Oil Colors and tubes, Water Colors in cakes and boxes, Brushes, Pallettes and Knives, Easels and Stretchers, Oil, Varnishes, Drawing Pens, Tacks, &c. Gilt and Rosewood Mouldings. Frames made to order at short notice.

Also, a fine stock of Paintings, Oil Prints, Engravings, Lithographs, colored and plain. Stereoscopes and Views, Globes, Writing Desks, Portfolios, Musical Instruments, Strings for Violin and Guitar of the first quality.

Cutlery of the best manufacture, Sheffield Knives, Razors, Strops, &c. ; Inks—black, blue and carmine, Indellible and Copying; Copying Presses and their accompaniments, Mucilage, Chess and Backgammon Men and Boards, in great variety.

Fancy Articles too numerous to mention.

Arrangements having been made, he will obtain to order any book published in America or Europe. All new publications received as soon as issued, and sold at publisher's prices.

Wholesale Purchasers, Schools and Libraries supplied. Special attention given to all orders.   Address

P. B. GLASS,
Successor to R. L. BRYAN,
175 RICHARDSON STREET,
Columbia, S. C.

BOOKS FOR THE GARDEN AND THE FIELD.

FOR SALE BY P. B. GLASS.

The American Cattle Doctor, by G. H. Dodd, M. D., ... $1 00
The Field Book of Manures, by D. Jay Brown, 1 25
Sheep Husbandry, by Henry S. Randall...... 1 25
The Farmer at Home, by John L. Blake........ 1 25
Allen on the Culture of the Grape 1 00
Johnston's Agricultural Chemistry............... 1 25
The American Poultry Yard, by D. J. Browne, 1 00
The Orchard, with colored plates.................. 8 00
The American Fruit Culturist, illustrated....... 1 25
Youatt on the Horse.........................$1 50   1 25
   "   "   Pig.......................................   1 25
   "   "   Sheep..................................   75
   "   "   Dog, ...$1 50   1 25
Buist's Family Kitchen Gardener.................   75
Stephens' Book of the Farm, 2 vols...............   4 00
Allen's American Farm Book...... . ...   1 00
Hand Books of Rural and Domestic Economy, as follows: The Hive and Honey Bee, Domestic Fowls, the Horse, Hogs, the Rose, the the Pests of the Farm, Essay on Manures, the Bird Fancier, the Cow, &c., each.........   25
Mason's Farming and Stud Book, by J. S. Skinner 1 00
Ornamental and Domestic Poultry, by Dixon & Kerr..... ....   1 00
The Fruit, Flower and Kitchen Garden, by S. Neill, LL. D.................... ....   1 25

Downing—Fruit and Fruit Trees of America...   1 25
  " Landscape Gardening..................   3 50
  " Country House...........................   4 00
The Fruit Garden, by P. Barns................   1 25
Buist's Rose Manual............................   75
  " American Flower Garden.................   1 25
Loudon on Gardening.............................   8 00
  " Encyclopœdia of Agriculture.........   8 00
The Muck Manual, by S. L. Dana...............   1 00
Buist's American Flower Garden Directory.....   1 25
Ladies' Southern Florist, or every Lady her own
 Flower Culturist, by Mary C. Rion; a supe-
 rior work, and complete Flower Garden Com-
 panion and Directory...........................   1 00
Kemp on Landscape Gardening 2 00
Paxton's Botanical Dictionary....................   7 00
American Weeds and Useful Plants.............   1 50
The Wheat Plant, &c., by J. K. Kleppart......   1 50
Domestic Fowls..................................   25
Cranford on Sheep...............................   50
Saxton's Rural Hand Books, 2 vols..............   3 00
Field Sports, by Frank Forrester, 2 vols.........   4 00
Stable and Table Talk............................   1 00
The American Angler's Guide.....................   1 50
Norton's Elements of Scientific Agriculture.....   60
Field's Pear Culture..............................   75
Sorgho and Imphee...............................   1 00
The Cotton Planter's Manual, by J. A. Turner   1 00
Pardee on Strawberry Culture....................   60
Munn's Practical Land Drainer..................   50
Flint on Grasses..................................   1 25
  " Milch Cows..............................   1 50
Warner on Hedges and Evergreens..............   1 00
 ☞ Besides the above mentioned, a large stock of
Agricultural, Horticultural, and Floricultural Works
are kept constantly on hand.

The Ladies' Southern Florist.

By MARY C. RION, of Winnsboro', S. C. 1 vol.,
12mo., handsome embossed cloth. Price, $1.
Columbia: Published by P. B. GLASS.

Extract from the Author's Preface.

The Author of this volume, desiring a book on
Flower Gardening which might be adapted to the
South, and, at the same time, written in such a manner as to be intelligible to one not a *professional Florist,*
was unable to find any work answering either of these
requisites. After procuring such works on Flowers as
were accessible, I commenced making memorandums
of such information as I found in these, by observation,
to be suited to our climate—making such modifications,
corrections and additions as my experience suggested.
These memorandums I enlarged by inquiries made of
practical flower-garden *workmen,* and by hints derived
solely from my own practice.

From the Yorkville Enquirer, July 19, Mr. DAVIDSON, *Contributing Editor.*

" It deals in actualities—not in sentimentalities about roses,
loves, angels and such stuff, of the fashionable poets. It tells in
plain language how to plant flowers, when and where; how to
dig, trench, hoe, manure, prune and water the flowers; how to
kill bugs, caterpillars and worms; how to manage cuttings, buddings, and hundreds of other similar things. There is fifty times
as much common sense in this little book on flowers—on *Southern*
flowers, be it remembered—as we have ever seen in anything of
the kind. We have gone ourself to the books for facts on flowers, and we speak from our observation. *The books* are far too
ambitious—they are up in the skies of science, in the clouds of
sentiment, but never down in the soil of practical facts. We
have seen volumes read upon some favorite but sickly climber,
which, meanwhile, died very quietly; all for want of some simple *home* truth too humble for *the books,* but which you can find
given in unmistakable language here in Mrs. Rion's 'Southern
Florist.'"

The "FLORIST" will be sent to any address, free of
postage, on receipt of $1.

SUGGESTED READINGS ON SOUTHERN GARDENS/PLANTS

Briggs, Loutrel W. *Charleston Gardens.* Photos by R. Adamson Brown et al. Columbia: University of South Carolina Press, 1951.

Hedrick, U. P. *A History of Horticulture in America to 1860.* New York: Oxford University Press, 1950. Reprint, with an addendum of books published 1861–1920, Portland: Timber Press, 1988.

Kibler, James. *On Reclaiming a Southern Antebellum Garden Heritage: An Introduction to Pomaria Nurseries, 1840–1879.* Original and photocopy. Columbia: South Caroliniana Library, University of South Carolina. Reprinted in *Magnolia: Bulletin of the Southern Garden History Society* 10, no. 1 (Fall 1993): 1–12.

Lockwood, Alice B., comp. and ed. *Gardens of Colony and State; Gardens and Gardeners of the American Colonies and of the Republic before 1840.* 2 vols. New York: Published for the Garden Club of America by C. Scribner's Sons, 1931–1934.

Meriwether, Margaret Babcock, ed. *The Carolinian Florist of Governor John Drayton of South Carolina . . . with Water-color Illustrations from the Author's Original Manuscript and an Autobiographical Introduction.* Columbia: South Caroliniana Library, University of South Carolina, 1943.

Porcher, Francis Peyre. *Resources of the Southern Fields and Forests, Medical, Economical, and Agricultural . . .* Richmond: West and Johnston, 1863.

Sarudy, Barbara Wells. "South Carolina Seed Merchants and Nurserymen before 1820." *Magnolia: Bulletin of the Southern Garden History Society* 8, no. 3 (Winter 1992): 6–10.

Shaffer, E. T. H. *Carolina Gardens*. New York: Devin-Adair Co., 1963.

Summer, William. *Descriptive Catalogue of Southern and Acclimated Fruit Trees, Evergreens, . . . Cultivated and for Sale at the Pomaria Nurseries*. Columbia: South Caroliniana Library, University of South Carolina.

Thornton, Phineas. *The Southern Gardener and Receipt Book*. Philadelphia: J. B. Lippincott, 1859.

Welch, William, and Greg Grant. *The Southern Heirloom Garden*. Dallas: Taylor Publishing Company, 1995.

White, William N. *Gardening for the South*. New York: C. M. Saxton, 1856.